YouTube
WORLD
RECORDS

DON'T TRY THIS AT HOME

Some of this book's clips feature stunts performed either by professionals or under the supervision of professionals. Accordingly the publishers must insist that no one attempt to re-create or re-enact any stunt or activity performed on the featured videos.

Published in 2020 by Welbeck

An Imprint of Welbeck Non-Fiction Limited, part of Welbeck Publishing Group.

20 Mortimer Street London W1T 3JW

Text © Welbeck Non-Fiction Limited, part of Welbeck Publishing Group.

A CIP catalogue record for this book is available from the British Library

Project Editor: Ross Hamilton
Design: Russell Knowles
Picture Research: Steve Behan
Production: Rachel Burgess

ISBN 978-1-78739-457-5

Printed in Dubai

10 9 8 7 6 5 4 3 2 1

YouTube
WORLD
RECORDS

ADRIAN BESLEY

WELBECK

CONTENTS

Introduction · 06

High-Flying Records · · · · · · · · · · · · · · · · · 08
Highs and Lows · 10
YouTube Hits Records · · · · · · · · · · · · · · · 12
Speed and Accuracy · · · · · · · · · · · · · · · · 14
The Need for Speed! · · · · · · · · · · · · · · · · 16
Extreme Weather · · · · · · · · · · · · · · · · · · · 18
Amazing Animal Records · · · · · · · · · · · · · 20
Freaky Food Records · · · · · · · · · · · · · · · · 22
Record-Breaking People · · · · · · · · · · · · · 24
Wild and Wacky · 26
Sports Record Breakers · · · · · · · · · · · · · · 28
Theme Park Records · · · · · · · · · · · · · · · · 30
Scary and Shocking! · · · · · · · · · · · · · · · · 32
Don't Try This at Home! · · · · · · · · · · · · · 34
Thirst-Quenching Records · · · · · · · · · · · · 36
The Biggest! · 38
The More, the Merrier! · · · · · · · · · · · · · · 40
Wild Weather Records · · · · · · · · · · · · · · · 42
Extreme Sports Records · · · · · · · · · · · · · 44
Super Sports Stars · · · · · · · · · · · · · · · · · · 48
Pure Strength · 50
Backwards Records · · · · · · · · · · · · · · · · · 54
Totally Gross! · 56
Multiple Record Holders · · · · · · · · · · · · · 58
Brilliant Buildings · · · · · · · · · · · · · · · · · · 60
Super-Fast Records · · · · · · · · · · · · · · · · · 64
Sound and Vision · · · · · · · · · · · · · · · · · · · 66
Crazy Critters · 68
Amazing Food Records · · · · · · · · · · · · · · 70
Super Strength Records · · · · · · · · · · · · · 72
Holding Out for a Hero · · · · · · · · · · · · · 74
Totally Different · · · · · · · · · · · · · · · · · 76
Cool Cat Records · · · · · · · · · · · · 78

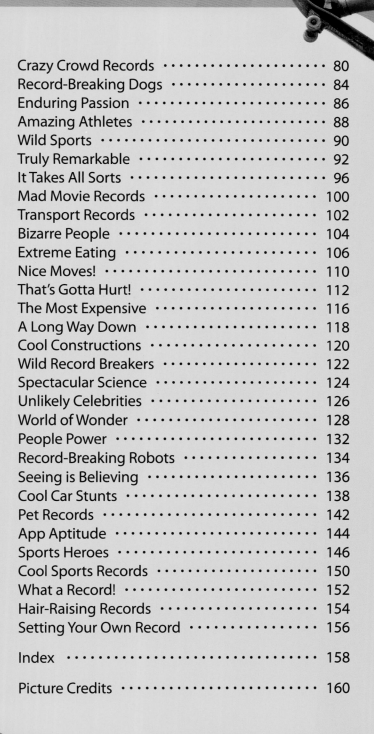

Crazy Crowd Records · 80
Record-Breaking Dogs · · · · · · · · · · · · · · · · · · 84
Enduring Passion · 86
Amazing Athletes · 88
Wild Sports · 90
Truly Remarkable · 92
It Takes All Sorts · 96
Mad Movie Records · · · · · · · · · · · · · · · · · · · 100
Transport Records · 102
Bizarre People · 104
Extreme Eating · 106
Nice Moves! · 110
That's Gotta Hurt! · 112
The Most Expensive · · · · · · · · · · · · · · · · · · · 116
A Long Way Down · 118
Cool Constructions · · · · · · · · · · · · · · · · · · · 120
Wild Record Breakers · · · · · · · · · · · · · · · · · 122
Spectacular Science · · · · · · · · · · · · · · · · · · 124
Unlikely Celebrities · · · · · · · · · · · · · · · · · · · 126
World of Wonder · 128
People Power · 132
Record-Breaking Robots · · · · · · · · · · · · · · · 134
Seeing is Believing · · · · · · · · · · · · · · · · · · · 136
Cool Car Stunts · 138
Pet Records · 142
App Aptitude · 144
Sports Heroes · 146
Cool Sports Records · · · · · · · · · · · · · · · · · · 150
What a Record! · 152
Hair-Raising Records · · · · · · · · · · · · · · · · · · 154
Setting Your Own Record · · · · · · · · · · · · · · 156

Index · 158

Picture Credits · 160

INTRODUCTION

Welcome to the only records book that enables you to see the records being broken for yourself. Enter the short URL or scan the QR code into your phone, tablet, laptop or computer and witness history being made across the world.

The fastest, biggest, highest, thinnest – all over the world people are united by a fascination with extraordinary achievements. We all love a record breaker. Whether it is a hundredth of a second being shaved off a famous sporting record or the first recording of a fantastically bizarre new category, we share a love of discovering who and what. Till now, the only thing missing has been our chance to actually see the record-breakers in action…

That's where YouTube comes in. This global resource is open to anyone to upload their videos. It contains literally thousands of record-breaking clips, from the most well-known to the completely obscure. Some have millions of views, while others remain virtually undiscovered.

Among the gems available to view are the tallest bonfire in the world; the longest time spent by a human in virtual reality; the fastest speed reached by a human in an Iron Man-esque jet suit; the world's most prolific competitive eater; a woman with the world's strongest hair; and a miniature dog the size of a soda can!

This book is your guide to the best of the record-breaking videos on YouTube. It leads you to the most exciting, the most thrilling, the most interesting and the most ridiculous videos on the site. Just read through the brief description and then use the short URL address or the QR code to access the clip – all, of course, completely for free.

HIGH-FLYING RECORDS

Don't look down! It's time to meet some of the sky-high heroes of the record-breaking world. These are some vertigo-immune daredevils who don't know the meaning of fear.

The Wing King

http://y2u.be/eHPZPNzJwLA

On a hot day in May 2017, Fraser Corsan jumped from a plane, 35,508 feet (10,823 metres) above the Californian desert. It's minus 137 degrees Celsius and all he's wearing is a wingsuit, but Fraser is a man on a mission. He was aiming to break a handful of records, but atmospheric conditions have limited him to one: pure speed. On exiting the plane, Fraser immediately hit a speed of 249 mph. He was going so fast that he saw cars going backwards on a motorway, five miles (8 kilometres) directly below him – fast enough to make him the world's fastest unassisted human.

WORLD'S FASTEST HUMAN

MOST ROPE JUMPERS TOGETHER

◀ 1,2,3... Jump

http://y2u.be/6SvExJadB78

When your mum says, "And if all your friends jumped off a bridge, would you do it too?" show her this clip. There are 245 of them, many of them probably friends, on a bridge in Hortolandia, near Sao Paulo, Brazil. On the signal, they all jump together from the 98-foot (30-metre) high bridge. Oh, and they're bound together and suspended from the bridge with rope. These thrill-seekers are not bungee jumpers but rope jumpers – their supporting lines having no elasticity – and never before have so many leapt into the unknown en masse.

Basket Case

https://youtu.be/evMG2atXH2c

Basketball legend and Harlem Globetrotter Hammer Harrison stands 6 foot 9 inches (2.6 metres) tall, so he already nets from quite a height, but here he ascends to 13,000 feet (4 kilometres) in a light aircraft, skydives and attempts a slam dunk. This might be the stuff hoop dreams are made of, but when he's in freefall he's travelling at 120 mph (190 km/h)? Surely, he's mad to attempt such a feat? After all, he's only got one shot at it – and he hasn't even got a helmet on.

▶

Over the Edge

http://y2u.be/QQzdakJQ-Mg

Imagine taking a leap from, say, the top of the Leaning Tower of Pisa, past jagged rocks and into a small pool beneath. In August 2015, in a world-record cliff-jump attempt, Brazilian-born daredevil Laso Schaller plunged almost 200 feet (60 metres) from a ledge into Switzerland's famed Cascata del Salto waterfall. Six oxygen tents were aerating the water in order to give him a softer landing, but Schaller hit the water outside of his intended landing zone – at a speed of around 76 mph (123 km/h). This high-quality video shows the death-defying jump from every angle, including the view from a camera mounted to his helmet.

HIGHS AND LOWS

These record-breakers have gone to extreme heights (or as low as they can go) in order to get their names in the record-books.

▼ Skate Limbo

http://y2u.be/7HEPRZuRWvc

Like many young kids, Gagan Satish, a Bangalore schoolboy, loves to get out on his rollerskates. Not many have a talent like Gagan's though. He skated nearly 230 feet (70 metres) with his face just 5 inches (12.7 centimetres) from the ground – passing under 39 cars on the way! Gagan has only been rollerskating for three years, but, even more incredibly, he is only six-years-old. Obviously, his experience helped him break the record; the previous holder was only five!

CHAMPION LIMBO ROLLER SKATER

Breathtaking!

http://y2u.be/YtryV9qltsg

Next time you're at your local swimming pool, see how long you can hold your breath underwater. Can you do 30 seconds? Or maybe 45, if you really fill your lungs? This exercise will give you some appreciation of Canadian William Winram's 2013 record dive into the Dead Sea at Sharm el-Sheikh in Egypt. Will took a single breath and held it for 3 minutes and 8 seconds, using a sled to help him descend 475 feet (145 metres) – for comparison, New York's Statue of Liberty is just 300 feet (92 metres) high – and a rope and monofin to speed his return to the surface.

WORLD RECORD FOR HIGHEST FREE SLACKLINING

Fine Line

https://youtu.be/ySzYnwJ6JqU

To mark 872 years since the founding of Moscow, these tightrope walkers have taken celebrations to new heights. Those on the ground can only stand, stare and hold their breath as a group of international tightrope walkers attempt to cross a wire stretched between two of the city's tallest skyscrapers. The wire is over 800 feet (245 metres) long and at a height of 1,150 feet (350 metres). It's clearly quite windy up there and the sky-walkers don't appear to be wearing harnesses, so it's incredibly tense, particularly when one of the them casually stops in mid-air to spread some love!

1,100-FOOT HIGH TIGHTROPE

▲ No Slacking

http://y2u.be/p-6RHjC_SvE

Is tightrope walking a little too safe for you? Try slacklining – walking across flexible, rubber band-type webbing. Still no rush? Then highlining is for you. That's slacklining hundreds, or even thousands, of feet above ground. This beautifully shot video featuring Friedi Kühne's world record longest free solo slackline lasts 38 seconds, but perfectly captures the adrenaline appeal and danger of the sport. 'Free' means walking without a safety harness, but Friedi seems fearless as he walks a 328-foot (110-metre) line over the 656-foot (200-metre) high Verdon Gorge, in the Alpes-de-Haute-Provence in the South of France.

YOUTUBE HITS RECORDS

In just over 10 years, YouTube has grown to be a part of the daily lives of millions of people. No surprise, then, that it now has its own illustrious record-holders.

▶ K-pop Kings

https://youtu.be/pBuZEGYXA6E

YOUTUBE'S MOST WATCHED VIDEO

The seven-member Korean boy band BTS have become a global phenomenon, smashing every possible record for a K-pop group. In 2017 they moved beyond K-pop when their fans – known as "ARMY" – set the record for the most Twitter engagements, with an average of 252,200 retweets per tweet. Then, in 2018, BTS went a step further, as this video for the band's track "Idol" set a YouTube record for most views in 24 hours, beating out Taylor Swift's "Look What You Made Me Do" by amassing an amazing 45 million views in one day.

◀ What a Marvel

https://youtu.be/TcMBFSGVi1c

Within 24 hours of its worldwide release in March 2019, the second official trailer for Marvel Studios' *Avengers: Endgame* received 268 million views. At the time of writing, only one trailer had been watched more in its first 24 hours – the first official trailer for the same movie, which was viewed 289 million times. It seems safe to say that the forthcoming film was eagerly anticipated, which is probably why it ended up earning $2.8 billion at the box office, making it the second highest grossing movie of all time.

Reality Check

http://y2u.be/lVaBvyzuypw

The future has arrived – again. Virtual reality is here. For mere pocket money you can buy a cardboard set that enables you to enjoy a simulated physical presence in a virtual or imaginary environment. And it's those innovative popsters, Gorillaz, who've made the biggest splash. Their surreal 360° virtual-reality video for the track "Saturnz Barz" picked up 7 million views in just one month, a YouTube record for the biggest debut of a VR video. However, with music and corporate big hitters about to dip their toes in the VR stream, this is one record that may not last long.

Charlie Still Bites

http://y2u.be/_OBlgSz8sSM

YouTube charts these days are dominated by music videos and children's TV shows, but one great exception refuses to die. In May 2007, a 56-second video of a young boy and his baby brother sitting side by side was posted on YouTube. 'Charlie Bit My Finger – Again!' became a YouTube phenomenon. It was sweet, cheeky and full of infectious laughter, and for years it competed with Miley, Justin and Taylor at the top of the viewing charts. Even now – with around 850 million views – it continues to be the most-watched "home video" on the site – the greatest viral video of them all.

▲ Listen to TED

http://y2u.be/_QdPW8JrYzQ

MOST WATCHED TED TALK EVER

TED talks have become a YouTube institution. The talks, which tend to last around 10 minutes, span every genre and are entertaining, often fascinating, always expertly delivered and a complete treat for the curious. Some are given by familiar names, such as Stephen Hawking or Bill Gates; others by academics, business leaders and politicians. This is the most popular TED talk ever. It features British stand-up comedian James Veitch giving a laugh-aloud talk entitled, 'This is what happens when you reply to spam email'. So far it has garnered 17 million views – 3 million more than any other TED talk.

SPEED AND ACCURACY

Another selection of quick-on-the-draw records. Here accuracy is just as important as speed: one false move could mean death, a dodgy haircut or a customer questioning their receipt.

▶ A Long Shot

https://youtu.be/trW9rxpSBxA

The Australian YouTube team, How Ridiculous, have made an art of breaking records – especially the highest basketball shot, which they have repeatedly broken. Their latest attempt took place at the spectacular Maletsunyane Falls in Lesotho, Africa, where the huge gorge provided the perfect drop zone. Watch as the ball sails through the air for an astounding 660 feet (201 metres) before dropping through the net without touching the sides. It looks easy, but the three Aussies spent eight hours a day for six days attempting the world record shot. They estimated they had attempted around 800 shots without success.

▶ Join the Club

http://y2u.be/6MGIlE2UIlI

Yeah, juggling – I know. It's definitely the most boring of circus skills, but put your prejudice aside and watch this guy in action because it's pretty amazing. In September 2016, before busy rail commuters at Toronto's Union Station, Cirque du Soleil's Rudolf Janecek became the fastest five-club juggler in the world. In a whirl of silver clubs and lightning hands, Rudolph shuffles along as he completes 429 rotations over 30 seconds. In fact, Rudolf threw and caught the clubs so fast that the adjudicators had to review the video in slow-motion before awarding him the record.

FASTEST CLuB JuGGLER

▶ Ploughing Ahead

https://youtu.be/h1DML_hlJhk

You wouldn't mind being stuck behind a tractor on a country lane if Guy Martin was in the driving seat. We know the man can ride motorcycles, tinker about under the bonnet and present TV shows, but we didn't know he could drive farm vehicles – at top speed. Here, in a rather damp field in northern England, he slips behind the wheel of a shiny, yellow JCB and puts his foot down to go for the fastest tractor record. Can he beat his previous run of 103 mph (166 km/h)?

▼ Crack the Whip

http://y2u.be/C9FsGHM6AaY

THE FASTEST WHIPPER IN THE WORLD

Indiana Jones eat your heart out. Nathan 'Whippy' Griggs is the whip king of the world and has the records to prove it. He holds the fastest records with both one and two hands, and possesses the longest whip in the world at over 329 feet 7.5 inches (100 metres) long (you can see that on YouTube too – check the sidebar). Wielding 6-foot 7-inch (2-metre) whips made of kangaroo leather, Nathan demonstrates stamina, skill and incredible co-ordination as he amasses 614 cracks in a minute using two whips. And, in case you're interested, that crack you hear is the whip breaking the sound barrier – over 750 mph (1,200 km/h).

A Brush with Fame

http://y2u.be/eXPJo1f60j0

Like most children, Dipanshu Mishra was probably told to clean his teeth at least twice a day. Now I'm sure Dipanshu always polishes up his pearly whites diligently, but he's also been practising with the brush to earn his place among the record breakers. His is a strange record, but one that is oddly compelling to watch, for Dipanshu balances a spinning basketball on the end of his toothbrush – and he keeps it spinning for an astonishing 42.92 seconds. That's quite a feat, especially considering he doesn't even play basketball!

THE NEED FOR SPEED!

Whoosh! There's no substitute for pure lightning strike speed and these guys have all taken the needle into the red with power, guts and a little madness …

▶ Lightning Bolt

http://y2u.be/4gUW1JikaxQ

"I am trying to be one of the greatest, to be among Ali and Pelé," said Usain Bolt, prior to competing in his final Olympics. That he was going to succeed was never in doubt. Usain Bolt is the fastest human being ever timed, with a list of world records as long as his magnificent, striding legs. At the Rio 2016 games Bolt won gold in the 100 metres, the 200 metres and the 4x100-metre relay. That meant he'd earned three gold medals at three consecutive Olympics and completed a "triple-triple". Truly a living legend.

THE FASTEST 100M SPRINT ON RECORD

▶ Revved Up

https://youtu.be/E6aHQD1UqoQ

From a standing start, how quickly can driver Sonny Persson, strapped into a sleek, red and black, high-performance Koenigsegg Regera, reach a speed of just under 250 mph (400 km/h)? An airstrip deep in the pine forests of Råda, Sweden, is the setting for this world record attempt. The acceleration is extraordinary – the trackside grass is a blur – and to a pounding soundtrack he hits the top speed in just 31.49 seconds or a shade over half a minute. This is genuine high-octane excitement!

▼ Splash Dash

http://y2u.be/sAubG28uODM

As speed records go, driving at 54 mph (87 km/h) isn't very fast. Except Gudbjørn Grimsson is driving on water. In an extreme Formula Offroad race in Iceland, the local driver took his suitably named Insane Racing buggy through the mud and drove over 1,000 feet (300 metres) down the river. With huge-treaded tyres acting like scoops on a paddle steamer, the buggy skims along on the water. To generate enough power, the car has four-wheel drive and a 1,600 horsepower twin-turbo engine. So probably best not to try it in the family estate car then.

THE FASTEST CAR ON WATER

▼ Run For It

https://youtu.be/A73HQwEct-o

You might remember this historic feat, because it made headline news around the world, and if you do (spoiler alert!) you will know that Eliud Kipchoge did indeed run a marathon in under three hours – in an incredible 1:59:40 to be precise. You might also recall the pacers who surrounded Kipchoge like bodyguards, and were swapped out regularly to ensure they were fresh and that each mile was covered at the optimum speed. In fact, every element of the run was carefully controlled and this fascinating video tells the story of exactly how that was achieved.

Handstand Finish

http://y2u.be/9p8LZVZoUzk

Tameru Zegeye is known as "The Miracle Man of Ethiopia". Born with deformed feet and unable to use his legs, Tameru learned to walk on his hands. His agility earned him a place in a circus, but he has proved his athletic skills as well. While visiting the small town of Fürth in north Bavaria, Germany, the 32-year-old completed a 100-metre sprint on crutches in a world record time of 56 seconds. What is really amazing is Tameru's technique, an incredible gravity-defying combination of balance, strength and co-ordination.

EXTREME WEATHER

Witness the shock and devastation brought by these record-breaking natural disasters – hurricanes, tsunamis and other calamitous events – in tense and dramatic footage uploaded to YouTube.

▶ Weather Report

http://y2u.be/unV5KcSrY-I

This clip went viral and became known as the 'Hurricane Charley Gas Station' video. It shows a petrol station in Charlotte Harbor, Florida being torn apart by winds of over 155 mph (249 km/h). Hurricane Charley, classed as Category 4 (the second strongest band), was the strongest hurricane to hit southwest Florida for 50 years. These winds were the strongest ever caught on video and were captured by Mike Theiss, whose brilliant weather films appear on the Ultimate Chase channel.

The Super Tsunami

http://y2u.be/2uCZjqoRLjc

On 9 July 1958, an earthquake caused a landslide at the head of Lituya Bay in Alaska. It generated a mega-tsunami measuring between 100 feet (30 metres) and 300 feet (91 metres), the highest tsunami wave in recorded history. This fascinating four-minute BBC clip tells the story of the tsunami, illuminated by the work of scientists who have uncovered evidence of the destruction caused. It has been viewed more than two million times.

▶ Stone Me

https://youtu.be/a2HgD_guGGo

Hailstones are lumps of ice that form in the clouds and fall to the ground when they become too heavy. This normally occurs when they reach half a centimetre in diameter. However, hailstones are formed in volatile thunder clouds and strong up-drafts can mean that instead of falling they are carried up to the freezing top of the cloud and enlarged. On 8 February 2018 a freak 20-minute hailstorm battered towns in Cordoba, Argentina, with hailstones that caused holes in the ground, damaged houses and deposited one incredible record-breaking hailstone that measured 9 inches (23 centimetres).

THE LARGEST LANDSLIDE IN HISTORY

▲ Mount Devastation

http://y2u.be/IhU6jml6NY4

Mount St Helens is a volcano in the US state of Washington. In 1980 an earthquake caused the north face to slide away, creating the largest landslide ever recorded. The landslide triggered explosions that sent rocks, ash, volcanic gas and steam into the air at over 300 mph (483 km/h) and created a column of ash that reached more than 15 miles (24 kilometres) into the atmosphere in only 15 minutes. This video, created from a series of photographs, reveals the enormity of this colossal act of nature.

AMAZING ANIMAL RECORDS

The animal kingdom has its champions too. A safari through YouTube's wildlife clips reveals some fascinating and surprising records and some incredible footage from the wild world.

▶ Monkey Business

http://y2u.be/zsXP8qeFF6A

About 98 per cent of their genome is identical to humans, so it is not surprising that chimpanzees are regarded as the cleverest of animal species. They can make and use tools, hunt in organized groups and have shown they are capable of empathy, altruism and self-awareness. Over and above all this, they are adept at computer skills – and in the case of Ayumu, featured in this video, can beat a human at memory games.

CHIMP WITH A MEMORY SUPERIOR TO HuMANS

◀ Big Bug

http://y2u.be/tBaRwtzFBbo

The Maoris call it "the God of Ugly Things". Bit rude? Looking at a picture of the Giant Weta, you might think it's a little like a cricket and not really that unsightly, but see the insect in real life and – whoa! – it's the size of a rodent. Once common in New Zealand, the world's biggest insect is now believed to live only on Little Barrier Island, about 50 miles northeast of Auckland. Weighing more than a sparrow, this creature is too heavy to jump, let alone fly, but it can pack a nasty nip with its oversized pincers.

▼ Don't Have a Cow

http://y2u.be/JMWrXkLGCwA

The world's tallest cow ever officially recorded was Blosom, a female Holstein. She weighed in at a whopping height of 74.8 inches (190 centimetres) – that's over 6 feet tall! Blosom was first recognized by the Guinness World Records in Orangeville, Illinois, USA, in May 2014, but went on to receive another honour, World's Tallest Cow Ever, in 2015.

▶ Loud Hailer

https://youtu.be/dvK-DujvpSY

This video has an on-screen warning that advises you to move your headphones away from your ears. That's because this is the white bellbird. It lives in the mountains of north-eastern South America and it holds the record for the bird with the loudest call. The sound reverberates like a bell and is created by the male, who is pure white. This noisy creature has a wattle that wobbles when he warbles, and when he opens his beak, the volume hits 125 decibels, which is as loud as a pneumatic drill.

WORLD'S TALLEST COW

◀ Short Shark Shock

https://youtu.be/8raLJHzWqVA

Deep Blue is a real life Jaws. At 20 feet (6 metres) long, she's thought to be the largest great white shark ever caught on film and the 50-year-old beast (they can live past 70) was filmed by diving enthusiast Michael Maier off the coast of Guadalupe Island, Mexico. Now, shark attacks are rare, but if you're going to suffer an aquatic assault it is most likely to be at the teeth of a great white – so how brave is the guy in the diving suit who goes for a high five with the marvellous marauding creature?

FREAKY FOOD RECORDS

The world of food and drink showcases some marvellous records, including enormous vegetables, oversized fast food and a time-honoured crazy method of cracking open champagne bottles.

▶ Burger King

http://y2u.be/KQ0uDYdpHfs

Two all-beef patties, special sauce, lettuce, cheese, pickles, onions – on a sesame seed bun. It's what we all know as a McDonald's Big Mac. And Matt Stonie is going to eat 25 of these? In less than an hour? We're talking around 11 pounds (5 kilos) of fast food, packing a hefty 13,250 calories. Popular YouTuber Matt, however, is nothing if not dedicated to his cause and, after getting over the $120 damage to his credit card at the drive-thru, he settles gamely to the task. Have a look. It's an entertaining watch, but perhaps not best viewed on a full stomach.

Grim Reaper

http://y2u.be/3zhym9oUSGU

The "Carolina Reaper", a crossbreed between a Ghost chilli pepper and a Red Habanero pepper, has been rated as the world's hottest chilli pepper. It averages a 1,569,300 on the Scoville scale, making it over 900 times hotter than Tabasco sauce. There are enough chilli-eating videos on YouTube to show what excruciating results can occur, but despite that the Danish TV host, Bubber, is foolish enough to step up to the plate...

Super Sabre

http://y2u.be/k_vfg1dJito

Napoleon is reputed to have declared: "Champagne! In victory one deserves it; in defeat one needs it." It was his troops who first popularized "sabring" champagne bottles – severing the neck from the bottle with the flat edge of a sabre. It is a precise skill – cutting through the glass at an exact stress point – and is one perfected by Mitch Ancona as he opens a world record 34 bottles in a minute. An achievement worth celebrating.

◄ Onion King

http://y2u.be/ZCIfa3L0dtY

Tony Glover was named King of the Onions when he managed to produce a mighty onion weighing 18 pounds 11 ounces (8.5 kilograms). Using seeds bought from the previous record holder, Peter Glazebrook, Tony says it took nearly a year to grow his mighty specimen. He gives them nitrogen-rich food and ensures the humidity is just right. Giant onions have trebled in size since 1985 and word has it that the holy grail of onions – the 20-pounder (9 kilograms) – is just around the corner.

Gold Plated

https://youtu.be/1C3oTE0Px90

It's always good to try a new food, right, so native New Yorker Casey Neistat sets out to sample the speciality of Ainsworth's, a restaurant just a few blocks from his office. The dish may well be mouth-watering and it certainly comes with an eye-watering price tag of a thousand bucks. What is it? Chicken wings, but not just any old chicken wings. These chicken wings are coated and fried in genuine 24-carat gold dust. So do the wings pass the taste test for Casey and his friend Sean? Pull a chair up and watch.

RECORD-BREAKING PEOPLE

Those born at the extremes of the physical spectrum – the tallest, the smallest, etc. – have always held a special fascination. These clips reveal the human beings behind some of the statistics.

Big Mouth

https://youtu.be/9Q0nZOGTgAg

He can fit a satsuma, an apple or an orange in there. He can get his jaws around a drinks bottle or a tennis ball. Isaac Johnson, a 14-year-old from Minnesota, has the world's largest gape. When he opens his mouth, it's 3.6 inches (9.34 centimetres) wide. Being his dentist must be a breeze. And we know Isaac makes regular trips to the dentist, because he wears braces. Hope those braces aren't holding him back from getting his teeth into ever-bigger spherical objects, though.

THE WORLD'S TALLEST TEENAGER

▶ Towering Teen

http://y2u.be/hBq06yJYqLQ

Teenage growth spurts are a common phenomenon. One minute your nephew is a 4-foot 12-year-old and the next time you see him he's 14 and pushing 6 feet. American Broc Brown is something else, though. Because of a genetic disorder known as Sotos Syndrome, or cerebral gigantism, he's been growing up to 6 inches a year throughout his teens. Broc is now 19 and stands 7 feet 8 inches (2.33 metres) tall. About to leave "teenagerdom" behind, Broc is on course to become the world's tallest man. The current record is held by Turkish farmer Sultan Kosen, who stands at 8 feet 1 inch (2.46 metres).

◀ Animal Magnetism

http://y2u.be/rbUuzCRa3Ug

Former kick-boxing coach Etibar Elchyev from Georgia is known as "Magnetic Man". Ever since he discovered his ability to attract metal objects to his body, Etibar has been setting new records. Here, in December 2013, we find him putting spoons on his chest and back – 53 in total, a new world record. An excellent talent, but he must dread visiting the cafeteria. Scientists claim his skin is not magnetic but merely "sticky". Whatever ... he's still in a magnetic field of his own!

▶ Inseparable Brothers

http://y2u.be/gPcijt2WaIs

Twin brothers Ronnie and Donnie Galyon were born healthy in Dayton, Ohio, in October 1951. Joined at the waist, they each had arms, legs and separate hearts but shared a stomach and some organs. Sixty-three years later they were still joined and could celebrate being the oldest-ever conjoined twins, beating Italian brothers Giacomo and Giovanni Battista Tocci, who were born in 1877. The twins spent their lives from the age of four in circus sideshows but have now retired to live with their younger brother.

WILD AND WACKY

Hidden away in the nooks and corners of YouTube are some odd and eccentric records. Here are just a few ...

◢ Living Doll

http://y2u.be/mhcW_81GRsU

Now aged 33, Brazilian-born Briton Rodrigo Alves has been having cosmetic surgery for over 15 years. He has had 51 surgeries and more than 100 cosmetic procedures – an official world record – and has completely changed his appearance. His nickname is "Human Ken" (after Barbie's boyfriend) and he most recently underwent a CO_2 laser treatment that burned off the top layer of his skin to leave him with a porcelain-like, blemish-free complexion. Alves, who is set to appear in a TV series about real-life dolls, says he has no intention of stopping and plans even more cosmetic changes.

THE WORLD'S MOST DOLL-LIKE HUMAN

Cutting Edge

https://youtu.be/666v4d8tYU8

To achieve the record for the fastest acceleration from 0 to 100 mph (161 km/h) in a lawn mower, a lawn mower has to look like a lawn mower. This one, a Honda Mean Mower, is definitely a ride-on model, although to be honest it looks more like a mini racing car, but with stunt driver Jess Hawkins at the controls it's certainly fast, reaching the target speed in a mere 6.285 seconds. The machine also has to be able to cut grass, although sadly we don't see it in that sort of action here.

◀ Tattoo Love

http://y2u.be/QIULSyKlrGY

Couples need a shared interest and there's no prize for guessing Chuck Helmke and Charlotte Guttenberg's common passion. Chuck, aged 75, and Charlotte, a sprightly 65-year-old, met in a tattoo studio in 2006. Charlotte was just discovering the joys of body art, while Chuck had begun covering his body in ink five years earlier. Now they are officially the male and female most-tattooed senior citizens world record holders. Displaying a colourful array of intricate tattoos, both boast over 90 per cent body coverage, with even their shaved heads inked. There's not a lot anyone can do to beat that!

MOST-TATTOOED SENIOR CITIZENS

▶ Dead Cool

http://y2u.be/xtHzRjnoXKw

In November 2014 in Mexico City, 509 slightly scary-looking skeletons in ball gowns and brimmed hats gathered in the city centre to set the world record for the largest gathering of Catrinas. The figure of Catrina, known as the Elegant Death, was created and immortalized in works by artists Guadalupe Posada and Diego Rivera and is now a traditional part of Mexico's Day of the Dead celebrations. People dress as the skeletal character to visit cemeteries and share offerings and food with the dead and their families.

A RECORD GATHERING OF CATRINAS

SPORTS RECORD BREAKERS

There's more to sport than winning. There are records to be broken. These athletes have etched their names in the history of their sports – however strange!

▶ All in a Day's Work

http://y2u.be/CQIk-aAHhFY

These days, breaking a record is as much about producing a great YouTube video as it is about performing the feat. The Face Team Acrobatic Sports Theatre of Hungary have certainly grasped that fact. They broke five world records in one day – the most basketball slam dunks by a team using a trampoline in one minute; the highest throw and catch of a spinning basketball; the farthest forward flip trampette slam dunk; the longest time spinning a basketball on a guitar; and the most passes of a spinning basketball in one minute (pair) – and captured it all in a fun three-minute video. Perfect.

Xtreme 19th

http://y2u.be/iOWR7O1oSgU

The Legend Golf 18-hole course in South Africa has a bonus hole – the "Xtreme 19th" – the highest and longest par three golf hole in the world. The tee sits on top of a cliff on Hanglip Mountain, more than 1,400 feet (427 metres) above a green carved in the shape of the continent of Africa – it takes nearly 30 seconds for the ball to hit the ground. Drill a hole-in-one and you win $1 million, but no one has yet bettered a two-shot birdie.

BEST LEAPING BASKET-BALLERS

28

► Kicking It

https://youtu.be/kdTR67GLeCc

Professional footballer Ederson De Moraes, goalkeeper for both Manchester City and the Brazilian national team, is known for hoofing the ball well into the opposition half, but can he break the record for the longest football drop kick? Not one for much of a warm-up (he says he doesn't like to run), he appears laid-back and relaxed. He takes a few practice shots then goes for it. He can have three attempts at the record. His first two fall just short of the record 246 feet (75 metres), so all rests on his third and final kick…

Hopping Mad!

https://youtu.be/L0nRle2oN54

The pogo stick has been a children's favourite for 80 years or so, but it only became the instrument of an extreme sport at the turn of the century. Supercharged springs and lightweight frames have made it a hopping cousin to the skateboard and BMX and the annual competition, Pogopalooza, which started in 2004, now attracts thousands of fans and the world's best pogoers. That's where the high jump world record is usually smashed, but this video features Biff Hutchison (who has broken multiple bones in his body coming off his stick) taking the prize in his own backyard. He cleared a bar set at an incredible 11 feet and half an inch (3.35 metres) high!

► Clogged Up

http://y2u.be/2CdYF41M6rw

Australian Rugby Union hero Drew Mitchell is his country's highest World Cup try scorer. However, the Toulon winger, who has played over 70 times for Australia, is also a serial record breaker. On the Sky Sports Rugby TV channel, he became joint holder of the records for both the most rugby passes and the most drop goals in a minute. He then set the record for the most apples crushed with the bicep in one minute (it was 14) and went on to perform this intriguing feat: the fastest 100 metres in clogs. Wearing the heavy wooden, Klomp-style clog common to the Netherlands, Drew hit the finish line in just 14.43 seconds.

FASTEST 100M WEARING CLOGS

THEME PARK RECORDS

Scream if you want to go faster! Actually, it isn't possible to go any faster than on some of these record-breaking rides – but you may find yourself screaming anyway.

FASTEST, LONGEST, TALLEST DIVE COASTER

▼ Gee Force

http://y2u.be/N79JKDtK4hg

What is it with you people? Sixteen million views? It's just a ride! The Zumanjaro: Drop of Doom, at the Six Flags Great Adventure in New Jersey, USA, is the tallest and fastest drop ride in the world. The eight-person gondola speeds to the top of the 415-foot (126-metre) structure in about 30 seconds, leaves them there a while to enjoy the view (or just exchange some nervous giggles) before rocketing them back down at 90 mph (145 km/h), reaching ground level again in less than 10 seconds – before they even have time to scream.

THE WORLD'S FASTEST DROP RIDE

Twist and Shout

https://youtu.be/V5rJVPSSoFs

Yukon Striker, which opened at Canada's Wonderland in Ontario in 2019, is 223 feet (68 metres) high, 3,625 feet (1,105 metres) long and has a maximum speed of 81 mph (130 km/h). It also has a 90-degree drop and four inversions, including a complete 360-degree loop, all of which makes it the world's tallest, longest and fastest dive coaster (a type of rollercoaster featuring a near-vertical drop). For maximum effect watch this POV video full screen, but to be on the safe side don't eat first!

▼ Slippery Slope

https://youtu.be/exxcazMTzAk

At least on YouTube you can enjoy this one without getting wet or worrying about drowning at the end. At just under 164 feet (50 metres), the Kilimanjaro water slide is the tallest body slide (one that doesn't require a raft) in the world. The slide at the Águas Quentes Country Club outside Rio de Janeiro, Brazil, takes a terrifying 60-foot (18-metre) drop into the pool way below. Apparently, nearly a third of those who reach the entrance are not brave enough to take the plunge, but those who do achieve speeds of over 60 mph (100 km/h).

Fast Formula

http://y2u.be/ijuQwnfBBZw

The Formula Rossa rollercoaster in Abu Dhabi's Ferrari World boasts acceleration from 0 to 60 mph (96 km/h) in just two seconds and reaches a world record 149 mph (240 km/h). In 2010, Felipe Massa and Fernando Alonso, Formula One motor-racing drivers, took their seats in the fastest rollercoaster on the planet. Now, while their bodies are used to being flung around at ridiculously high speeds, their faces are usually encased in helmets. Just watch as the G-force hits these seasoned speed merchants.

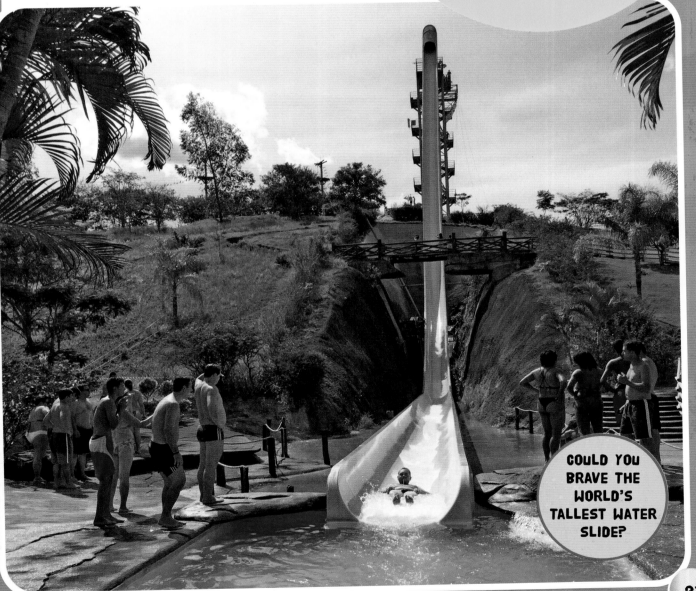

COULD YOU BRAVE THE WORLD'S TALLEST WATER SLIDE?

SCARY AND SHOCKING!

Delve into the lucky dip of the world of records and who knows what'll emerge. You could find some hair-raising danger, interesting collections and, sometimes, something truly, truly bizarre.

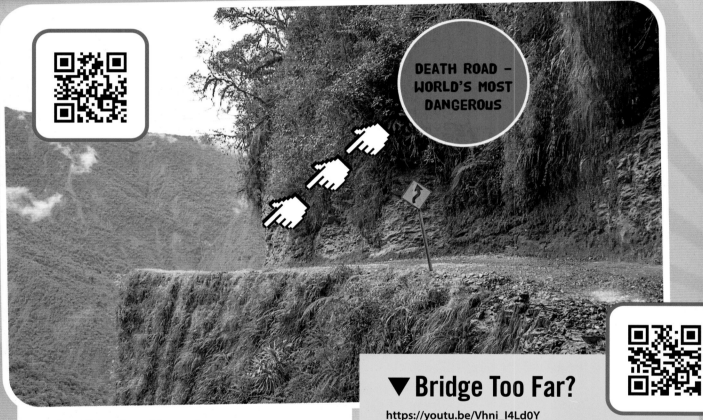

DEATH ROAD – WORLD'S MOST DANGEROUS

▲ Rocky Road

http://y2u.be/zGA3qXQs1wE

The North Yungas Road in Bolivia is 43 miles (69 kilometres) long and 2,000 feet (610 metres) high, and claims around 300 lives a year. No wonder it is called the Death Road. Perils along the Most Dangerous Road in the World include rock avalanches, fog and trucks squeezing by each other on its loose-stone surface. Often a single track 10 feet (3 metres) wide, it has no guard rails, just sheer drops down the cliff edges. The route does, however, offer some stunning scenery.

▼ Bridge Too Far?

https://youtu.be/Vhni_I4Ld0Y

It's very windy up on Ai-Petri, a peak in the Ukraine's Crimean Mountains, and it's also pretty foggy. However, you can take the cable car to the top and from there you can cross from rocky outcrop to rocky outcrop on a series of simple suspension bridges. No doubt walking through the clouds is an exhilarating experience, but the construction does look rather rickety – it's just a lot of short planks strung together with ropes for rails. Could this be the scariest set of bridges in the world?

Walk the Plank

http://y2u.be/KbtZfzxX44o

How far are you prepared to go for a breathtaking view? If you would happily walk along a seemingly rickety plank attached to the side of a mountain cliff hundreds of feet high, then Mount Huashan in China could be your ideal destination. The plankway doesn't lead anywhere – just to a stunning bird's-eye view of the surrounding mountains – and you have to return the same way, negotiating your way past those coming in the opposite direction. Overcome your fears, though, and you, too, can claim to have taken the world's most dangerous hiking trail.

Human Fireball

http://y2u.be/hICWU9HC7ts

Fire-protective clothing is available. It's worn by motor-racing drivers and movie stunt men. It's not for Anthony Britton, though. He dressed himself in three pairs of overalls, a few balaclavas and a motorcycle helmet for his attempt on the world record for fire running. Hundreds of spectators assembled in a park in Croydon, England, to watch Anthony, an experienced escapologist, soak himself in petrol, set himself on fire and run hell for leather across the grass. He completed an awesome 595 feet (181 metres) before calling in his team to douse the flames with fire extinguishers.

▶ Blown Away

http://y2u.be/AdtSdVop6V0

The James Bond franchise of movies has a long history of breaking a plethora of records. However, its latest achievement is arguably the most earth-shattering of them all. The climax of *Spectre*, the 24th Bond film in the series, featured the largest film-stunt explosion ever as Blofeld's desert base was detonated to kingdom come in front of the film's stars, Daniel Craig and Madeleine Swann. Shot on 29 June 2015 in Erfoud, Morocco, the blast used 2,224 gallons of fuel and 73 pounds (33 kilograms) of explosives. The sequence might have lasted just seven and a half seconds, but it was one memorable blast.

DON'T TRY THIS AT HOME!

How desperate can you be to get your name in the record books? These record breakers seem to feel no pain as they take one or more of their senses to the limit.

Candles in the Wind

http://y2u.be/kvGa-OXORhw

It's not big and it's not clever – though you have to admit it is kind of cool. File this in the not-to-try-at-home folder, but do take a look at 28-year-old Filipino Ronald Cabañas extinguishing 5 lit candles with his own bottom wind. In an extraordinary display of controlled flatulence, Ronald, using what can only be described as a home-made fart trumpet, puts out the candles in less than 30 seconds. It is a fine skill, but it's difficult to see how Ronald, a farmer and sometime porter, can make a career of it.

▶ Peg Face

http://y2u.be/pS2AszO0z44

GREATEST NUMBER OF PEGS ON FACE

We've all got a skill lurking somewhere, it's just a matter of finding it. Kelvin "The Peg Man" Mercado, 36 years old, discovered he had a unique talent for clipping clothes pegs on his face. Now he's a world-record holder. Pegs are attached in neat formation to every loose, and not so loose, piece of skin as well as to his lips and nose. Altogether he managed to clip on 163 pegs – and it makes for quite a sight.

▼ Saucy Drinker

http://y2u.be/bKxJKXA1LxM

The bartender in *Back to the Future Part III* refers to it as 'wake-up juice', but just the sight of the familiar jar of Tabasco sauce is enough to strike fear into the heart of many a diner. Its three simple ingredients - red peppers, salt and distilled vinegar - pack a punch measuring 2,500–5,000 SHU on the Scoville scale. Hats off then to the YouTuber known as the 'L.A. Beast' who is prepared to risk his dignity by downing an entire gallon of Tabasco in one go! Please DO NOT attempt to copy him…

▶ Fired Up

https://youtu.be/WQT1IVUrO2s

Bryan Miser is a human cannonball and the record-breaking 'Human Fuse'. Not only is he shot from a canon to land – with any luck – on a large inflatable, but as part of this process he is also set alight. This is Bryan's 2019 audition for *America's Got Talent* and as he flies through the air in flames you can really feel the tension. The audience were open-mouthed, but what do you think Simon Cowell and the other judges had to say?

Melon Madness

https://youtu.be/dx-j3WvAajc

Ashrita Furman has set more than 700 official Guinness Records since 1979 and currently holds more than 200 records in everything from underwater hula-hooping to catching ping-pong balls with chopsticks (32 in a minute!). This one has the added element of danger as we find Ashrita lying on his back and, wielding a razor-sharp machete, chopping as many watermelons in

half as he can in a minute – on his stomach! Don't even think about doing it! It's not even clear how he doesn't end up a bloody mess. Some might call him mad, but in the record-breaking world, Ashrita is a living legend.

A HUMAN CANNONBALL

THIRST-QUENCHING RECORDS

It's not just drinking the liquid stuff quickly (although, boy, can they guzzle!), but shaking it, sucking it, carrying it and performing all sorts of records with it!

Beer Duty

http://y2u.be/nALw8IOLDfw

Tax inspector by day, tankard carrier by beer festival, Oliver Strümpfel is a superhero in the bar-tending world. His personal arena is the Gillamoos Fair in Abensberg, Bavaria, where he is king of the *Maßkrugtragen* – the beer-stein carrying challenge. He took up the challenge to try to beat an Australian who reigned as the Meister of *Maßkrugtragen*. In 2010 he managed to beat him by carrying 21 tankards. In 2014 he took his record to 25. Following a nine-month gym regime, this is Strümpfel's 2017 attempt to extend his record even further.

Chug a Lug

https://youtu.be/x0f2mcgNUIk

Eric 'Badlands' Booker is a professional eater, rapper, and chugging specialist. He has a real talent for consuming fizzy liquids at top speed, but how quickly can he suck up five cans of delicious cranberry-flavoured Sprite? Well, it takes him longer to fill the large glass boot with his favourite soft drink than it does to down it, and his burp lasts almost as long as the chug itself, but it's a world record (at least, according to Eric it is) and certainly pretty impressive.

 ## Flip Out

http://y2u.be/INb2FChnoIQ

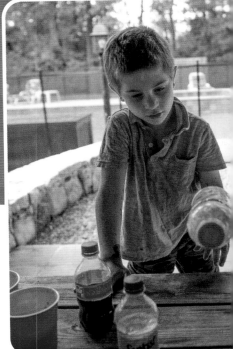

As 2017 began, bottle-flipping had reached epidemic proportions. Kids everywhere were flicking a partially filled plastic bottle in the hope it would land on its base. Schools banned the practice and Mike Senatore, the man whose viral video had launched the craze, went online to apologise for distracting the nation's youth. Out in Sweden, things became even crazier. With a 130-litre bottle supplied by supermarket chain Lidl, two YouTubers ventured to the middle of a bridge to attempt the world's biggest bottle flip...

CHAMPION BOTTLE-FLIPPER

▲ Straw Man

http://y2u.be/15BCllVcz38

As a child, Manoj Kumar Maharana dreamed of breaking a world record and, finally, as a 23-year-old, he fulfilled his ambition. He could have set out to win the Olympic 100 Metres or lift a car above his head, but instead he decided to beat Simon Elmore, a Brit who crammed 400 straws in his mouth in 2009. In 2017, Manoj managed to stuff an amazing 459 plastic drinking straws into his mouth at once, successfully keeping them there for the requisite 10 seconds without touching them.

Human Hydrant

http://y2u.be/U9_JFjZGkYA

There are over 600 muscles in the human body and many of them can be utilised to break a world record. Take Kirubel Yilma of Addis Ababa for example. He's a

medical student who put his knowledge of anatomy to use to achieve a record for spraying water from the mouth. He beat the existing record by 10 seconds as he squirted a continuous spray of water from his mouth for nearly a minute!

▼ Milking It

http://y2u.be/kBFugzV1Kxl

Kobayashi (also see page 107) shows his awesome power of consumption. Here he is at Uncle Bob's Self Storage in Upper Saddle River, New Jersey, tipping a gallon – that's eight pints! – of milk down his gullet in just 20 seconds. According to the clip's description, Kobayashi had set a record of eating 13 cupcakes in a minute, "so he needed to wash it down". Considering human stomachs are said to be able to contain around six pints, it's difficult to imagine where it is all going.

THE BIGGEST!

When it comes to record breaking, size is definitely important. The Biggest ... is always one of the most popular of the records categories. Here are a few colossal contributors ...

Right on Cue

http://y2u.be/dy6wkqRzc5I

When French billiards player Florian "Venom Trickshots" Kohler turned up in Las Vegas with a pool cue that was 17 feet and 7.4 inches (5.37 metres) long, he could hardly get it in the room. There was no doubt it was the longest pool cue ever but, to gain the record, Florian had to prove he could use it by breaking (splitting) the balls and then potting seven of them. As the weight of the cue was making it sag and bend in the middle, to secure that record the master player was going to have to use every last one of his silky skills...

▶ Cereal Killer

https://youtu.be/xRwy_rKc7gI

This challenge is much tougher than you might think and it starts with the world's largest cereal bowl, which is filled with 2,000 gallons (9,092 litres) of water, a lot of milk powder, and boxes and boxes of out-of-date breakfast cereal. It also involves cartoon creature costumes, rubber rings and four random members of the public. Whoever stays in the cereal bowl the longest wins $10,000. There's a great moment (among many) when one of the participants, running low on willpower and energy, asks for a granola bar.

WORLD'S LARGEST BOWL OF CEREAL

Big Game Boy

http://y2u.be/ezHsGggQEDg

The Nintendo Game Boy was a 1990s must-have device. This handheld console was the only way to play *Tetris* or *Super Mario* on the move. So forget your Xbox or PS4 – who wouldn't want a human-sized Game Boy? Belgian engineering student Ilhan Unal has entered the record books for creating the largest, fully functional Game Boy. The 21-year-old designed the giant console on his computer and then spent a month in a laboratory building it before wiring it to a normal Game Boy to enable it to play the original.

▼ Off the Wall

http://y2u.be/EptwF6cZMWg

Of all the records set in Brazil's Olympic year, this is the most eye-catching. Artist Eduardo Kobra designed a huge mural called *Etnias*, meaning "Ethnicities", on a wall of the Olympic Boulevard in Rio de Janeiro. The colourful spray-painted mural depicts the faces of indigenous people from five different continents. Using 180 buckets of acrylic paint and 3,500 cans of spray paint, the painting stands 51 feet (15.5 metres) high and stretches for 560 feet (170 metres). It's the largest spray-painted mural in the world, and it took Kobra and his team two months to complete.

THE WORLD'S BIGGEST MuRAL

THE MORE, THE MERRIER!

Ah, mass participation! A chance to meet other bizarrely dressed folk, to stretch your legs in unison or to smack each other around the head with a pillow!

▼ Zombie Apocalypse (almost)

http://y2u.be/QkqC6Fni2KE

They bill the Zombie Pub Crawl as the World's Greatest Undead Party with brain-eating competitions, live pop acts, a "Trapped in the Closet Sing-Along" and a zombie fun run! Minneapolis has been hosting the living dead (or people dressed up as them) annually since 2005. The original 500 zombies have multiplied until, in 2014, over 15,000 people were officially counted stumbling around in a stupefied manner. It was the official record for a zombie gathering.

▲ Pillow Talk

http://y2u.be/KQ_SYl9vlkc

Nobody wants to see fighting at a sports stadium, but maybe we can make an exception for CHS Field, the home of Minnesota baseball team St Paul Saints. At the end of the second inning of the Saints' match against the Winnipeg Goldeyes, a battle broke out – among all 6,261 of the spectators. This was a mass display of that friendliest of confrontations – the pillow fight. Provided with weapons by a local pillow company, the crowd, staff and mascots (although sadly not the players) attacked their neighbours with their night-time bolsters. It was the biggest pillow fight in the world – ever!

RECORD-BREAKING NUMBER OF ZOMBIES

▶ Under Attack

https://youtu.be/DCGDqQxmUDM

At Comic-Con in San Diego, California, in July 2019, fans of the Japanese anime TV series *Dragon Ball Z* set out to smash the world record for the largest number of people to perform the kamehameha (pronounced kah-may-ha-may-ha). The kamehameha is the first super energy attack – what you might call the signature move of the character Goku – and the previous record was 250. Fortunately, actor Sean Schemmel, who voices Goku, was on hand to warm up the 784-strong crowd and teach them how to get it just right.

◢ Packed Pillion

http://y2u.be/YwRafRr8dk4

The Indian Army has set a new world record for 58 men riding on a single motorbike. It's not a skill modern soldiers should need but, with defence-budget cuts common, you never know. The 500-cc Royal Enfield chugged along an Air Force runway and covered a distance of 0.75 miles (1.2 kilometres) with members of the Tornadoes, an army motorcycle display team, precariously balancing on either side. The stunt, which broke the Tornadoes' own record by four riders, involved six months' planning and training, military discipline and precision – and quite a lot of falling off.

MOST PEOPLE RIDING A SINGLE MOTORBIKE

Marvel-lous Meeting

https://youtu.be/USX0L_maReQ

Supervillains must have been running scared in the streets of the Swedish capital, Stockholm, in September 2018 at the sight of over 500 Spider-men. None of them were actually seen climbing buildings or shooting spider webs from their wrists, but all had the "spider sense" to turn up at Comic Con as Marvel and Sony attempted a world record for the largest number of costumed Spider-men gathered in one place. In the end, 547 of the ersatz superheroes left as brand-new record-breakers, but they would do well to heed the words of Peter Parker's Uncle Ben: "Remember, with great power comes great responsibility."

WILD WEATHER RECORDS

Mother Nature is a prodigious record breaker and produces some of the most spectacular events you can see on YouTube. Just watch the disintegrating iceberg, dramatic twister and other gripping footage on these pages.

Tip of the Iceberg

http://y2u.be/hC3VTgIPoGU

Over 20 million people have watched this amazing clip from the documentary *Chasing Ice*. The footage shows the historic breakup at the Ilulissat Glacier in western Greenland – the largest iceberg calving ever filmed. Glacial calving happens when an iceberg breaks off from the larger ice shelf, in this case a piece measuring 1.8 cubic miles (7.4 cubic kilometres). The Ilulissat (aka Jakobshavn) glacier produces around 10 per cent of all Greenland icebergs with around 35 billion tonnes of icebergs calving off every year.

▼ It's a Twister!

http://y2u.be/Q7X3fyId2U0

During the evening of 31 May 2013, the widest tornado in recorded history occurred over rural areas of central Oklahoma. It was 2.6 miles (4.2 kilometres) wide at its widest point and tracked across 16.2 miles (26 kilometres). The storm, with accompanying wind speeds of more than 295 mph (475 km/h), fortunately struck mostly in rural areas. Even so, eight people lost their lives as a result of the tornado. All of them were killed in vehicles – either they were trying to flee by outdriving the twister or they were storm chasers filming the cataclysmic event.

THE WIDEST TORNADO EVER RECORDED

RECORD-BREAKING LIGHTNING STORMS

▲ Everlasting Lightning

http://y2u.be/edrAL2t99kE

In 2014, an area of northwestern Venezuela, where the Catatumbo River meets Lake Maracaibo, was officially recognized as having the most frequent lightning storms. Known as Relámpago del Catatumbo – the Catatumbo Lightning – this "everlasting storm" appears almost every night. Averaging 28 lightning strikes per minute for up to 10 hours at a time, it can spark as many as 3,600 bolts in an hour. Although many myths surround the phenomenon, scientists claim it is just regular lightning, whose frequency can be explained by regional topography and wind patterns.

Chillsville, Siberia

http://y2u.be/gRbaAaJgW0A

Next time you feel a little chilly, spare a thought for the 500 or so inhabitants of Oymyakon, the coldest inhabited place on Earth. Oymyakon (the name ironically means "unfrozen water") is in north-eastern Siberia, a two-day drive from the world's coldest major city, Yakutsk, and just a few hundred miles from the Arctic Circle. It is pitch-black dark for up to 21 hours a day during the winter and the temperature averages -50° Celsius (-58° Fahrenheit). In 1933, it plunged to -68°C (-90°F). Get through that, though, and you can look forward to endless summer days and temperatures rising to a balmy 23°Celsius (73.4°F).

Haven't the Foggiest

https://youtu.be/nOfMTOj1wNc

Is Lark Harbour, a small fishing community on the western coast of the Canadian province of Newfoundland, the foggiest place in the world? It must surely be one of them, because when the fog rolls in from the sea it's like an enormous waterfall or an avalanche of fog. This video is shot looking up at the wall of fog, and it's cool but slightly scary. However, do click the link below to the video taken from further away, because that's awesome too.

EXTREME SPORTS RECORDS

There's danger out there on the streets. Especially if you are mad enough to try to go faster, higher, lower than anyone else in your chosen extreme sport.

Sacré Bleu!

http://y2u.be/MV2iURlttxo

French athlete Taig Khris is a hero of the inline skating world but is as well-known by the French public for skating off tall buildings. Having taken a plunge from the first floor of the Eiffel Tower In 2010, Khris now jumped from the Sacré-Coeur – the highest point in Paris. He flew down the 492-foot (150-metre) ramp, taking off with the whole city behind him, and soft-landed on an inflatable half-pipe. He set a new world distance record with a long jump of 95 feet (290 metres).

▼ Daring Descent

https://youtu.be/svfI-bTdMcl

Tianmen Mountain in China is a major tourist attraction, famous for its water-eroded cave and its flight of 999 stairs, but since 2017 it has also been home to the world's longest parkour course, which covers the entirety of the stairs. This video, which went viral and collected over 15 million views, was shot by 19-year-old Calen Chan as he vaulted down the course in just over two minutes. It's fabulously exciting and surprisingly well shot, as Chan didn't have a head or chest strap for his GoPro and filmed the descent with his camera in his mouth.

THE WORLD'S LONGEST PARKOUR COURSE

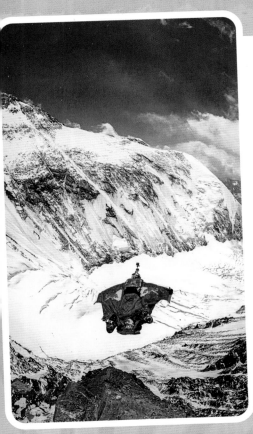

◀ Russian BASE Jumper

http://y2u.be/oQjp0DgqWpg

Russian extreme-sports star Valery Rozov endured a 31-day expedition to reach the site of his record-breaking BASE jump. In 2013, he had performed the highest-ever BASE jump on Mount Everest, but that wasn't enough for the adrenaline junkie. In 2016, he climbed to just below the summit of the sixth-highest mountain in the world, Cho Oyu in China, in an attempt to better his record. From a height of over 25,000 feet (7,700 metres), Valery leaped off the mountain, spending 90 seconds in free-fall before his parachute opened, and landing on a glacier 5,500 feet (1,700 metres) below and 11,500 feet (3,500 metres) away.

Mountain High

https://youtu.be/NEA0aGcbAVQ

Dani Arnold is a speed climber and in September 2019 he set a world record time for climbing the north face of the Cima Grande, a peak in the Dolomites in northern Italy, via the particularly challenging Comici route. The ascent took him 46 minutes and 30 seconds, but what was even more impressive is that Dani is a free climber, so he doesn't use equipment – no special boots, no ropes, just ordinary trainers and his bare hands. Absolutely terrifying!

▼ Back-Breaking Work

http://y2u.be/Z-OsL4eCgP0

Records don't just happen. New Zealand's Jed Mildon not only spent three intensive months training for his historic triple BMX backflip, but also had to build a super-ramp, 66 feet (20.12 metres) high, into a hillside in order to do it. Jed had kept his attempt to become the first-ever rider to perform three full backwards rotations secret before attempting it in front of 2,000 spectators. They watched spellbound as he careered down the long ramp, shot up a 11.8-foot (3.6-metre) super-kicker, became airborne and created history.

RECORD TRIPLE BACKFLIP

▼ Jet Set

https://youtu.be/y6VlzFj8LBQ

Richard Browning is wearing over-sized binoculars on his arms, a long orange skirt and weird cardboard fins on his ankles. He doesn't exactly look cool, the jet suit he invented really is. From beside the pier on the beach at Brighton on the UK's south coast, he zooms out over the sea at 85 mph (137 km/h), leaving a trail of sparks behind him. This makes him the holder of the world speed record in a jet suit. Way to go.

FASTEST JET-ENGINE POWER SUIT

SUPER SPORTS STARS

You don't have to be a big-time pro to be a sporting record breaker. A former NASA scientist, a teenage cheerleader and 6,000 students all wrote their name in the book in style.

WORLD'S LARGEST DODGEBALL GAME

Hop, Skip, Jump

https://youtu.be/kVHFc1RQ-HQ

This team of precision speed-skippers are Chinese middle school students. There are 12 of them. Ten of them jump very, very quickly, while the other two turn the rope, although that rope is going so fast you can barely see it. The girls link arms, the boys just lean in, but it's ridiculously intense. They are going after the record for the most simultaneous jumps over a single rope in one minute. It's like machine gun fire as they do 225 jumps. That's more than three and a half jumps per second.

▼ University Challenge

http://y2u.be/ZdkU4oDcp40

Forget Oxford and Cambridge or Harvard and Yale; the greatest university rivalry is between the University of California in Irvine and the University of Alberta in Canada. Since 2010, the two colleges have had a running battle to seal the record for the largest dodgeball game. Alberta were the first to make a mark with 1,198 players but since then the honours have swung back and forth. In 2012, in a game involving 6,084 participants, Irvine took the title, but who knows what the Canadians have planned?

Back in (Fast) Time

https://youtu.be/XVQCkM6X-Aw

Aaron Yoder from Kansas, USA, is going backwards fast. He holds the record for the fastest backward-running mile, stopping the clock at a ridiculous 5 minutes and 54 seconds. After a knee-injury stopped a promising forward-running career, Aaron started going backwards and turned to "retro-running". Now a recognized sport with its own World Championships, backwards running puts very little stress on the knee and various other joints (although you probably get the odd cricked neck!). In just over three years, Aaron had become the fastest backwards human over 200 metres, 1000 metres and the mile.

Tumble Turn

http://y2u.be/deJcMFDMjk0

You may not have heard of Angel Rice but, if power tumbling succeeds in becoming an Olympic sport, she will be a global celebrity. Power tumbling involves momentum and strength in a short series of twists and flips, and the 17-year-old is the USA team's star turn. Known as the "Queen of Tumbling", Angel has twice won the World Cheerleading Championships, but it has been her TV appearances that have brought her the most attention. After breaking the world record for tumbling in one minute on the *Today* show, she was up to her twisting tricks again with Steve Harvey.

▲ Putting It Right

http://y2u.be/htmbMSRj1SQ

Dave Pelz quit being a NASA scientist in 1976 to concentrate on his golf coaching. Using scientific methods, he became an expert in the "short game" – shots made from within around 100 yards of the hole. In 2004, his research paid off. Filming a TV segment for the Golf Channel during PGA Championship week at Whistling Straits in Kohler, Wisconsin, Pelz holed a 206-foot (62.79-metre) putt – beating broadcaster Terry Wogan's previous record of 33 yards (30.2 metres) at Gleneagles.

HIGHEST BASKET EVER MADE

◄ Thunder Strikes Again

http://y2u.be/Wnz4ok5GkZg

Harlem Globetrotters' Thunder Law is the team's designated record-breaker. Longest backwards shot (see page 54), longest basketball shot blindfolded, longest shot while sitting, and now highest upwards shot records have all fallen to the 6 feet and 3 inches (1.905-metre) tall player sporting the number 34. His latest entry in the record books came in 2017 in front of the grand staircase at the Utah State Capitol in Salt Lake City. A hoop was hung from a crane at a height of 50 feet and 1 inch (15.27 metres) and the result was surely never in doubt.

PURE STRENGTH

You won't see weights being lifted like this down the local gym. These guys pull, flip and lift in eye-watering feats of strength that just don't seem possible.

Bend an Ear

https://youtu.be/4E2WR_ZpD4w

Daredevil performer Johnny Strange set the record for lifting weights using just chains attached to his ears when he picked up 50 pounds (22.6 kilogrammes), the equivalent of a bicycle hanging from each ear, to earn himself the title of "the man with ears of steel" (you can see that on YouTube, too). Now you can't go around with a moniker like that without flaunting it, so here's Johnny again, this time pulling the heaviest weight ever – obviously with his ears – as he lugs a 1500-lb (680-kg) Cessna 172-P aircraft over 66 feet (20 metres).

Hook, Line and Sinker

http://y2u.be/WgGg0innugM

You don't get given the nickname "The Human Toolbox" for nothing. Among his sword-swallowing and bed-of-nails stunts, extreme entertainer Brad Byers is also given to inserting various items – nails, drill bits, hooks – into his head, usually through the nasal cavity. So, here's a warning: if you are squeamish, this video might not be for you. We see Brad insert a hook and pull along a full multi-person bicycle weighing nearly a ton. It's an obscure record but a mighty impressive one: The Heaviest Load Pulled from a Hook in the Head!

EXTREME HOOK INSERTIONS

THE WOMAN WHOSE STRENGTH IS HER HAIR

▼ Steel Yourself

http://y2u.be/k9rQAOp3xVQ

Amandeep Singh is the Indian Man of Steel – a guy who has immense body strength, seemingly feels no pain and is surely as mad as a box of frogs. Witness his show reel, where he makes his bid to be known as the World's Strongest Man. It's difficult not to wince as he retains a grip on ropes holding back 20 motorcyclists,

has a car run over his head and a full-sized truck run over his rear, and takes sledgehammer blows to his most sensitive body parts. Now that's gotta hurt!

A Smashing Time

http://y2u.be/LqisPXXqpEY

What do you do with those pumpkins once Halloween is over? It isn't a problem for Conor Murphy and his trusty tool. Watch him take a sledge hammer to a truckload of pumpkins; there is something immensely satisfying in such wanton destruction. The CrossFit coach from Boston, USA, makes swift work of pumpkin obliteration as he pounds his way through a record 30 orange gourds in just one minute. It's no mean feat. The guy is seriously fit and he not only secured the world record, but doubled the previous total. Now, who's for pumpkin soup?

▼ Letting Her Hair Down

http://y2u.be/YoBFYQiOCHE

Circus of Horrors star Anastasia IV (Joanna Sawicka from Wimbledon, London) is proud of her hair. She combs it for hours and washes it five

times a day. Anastasia isn't vain, she needs to do this to keep her record-breaking hair in top condition. Anastasia spends most of her stage show dangling from her hair, but also lifts record weights with her locks, lifts people, and, in this clip, pulls a 2.5-ton funeral hearse 65 feet 6 inches (20 metres) down the road in under four minutes.

▼ Quick Pit Fitters

https://youtu.be/Bl75uWxEajA

In Formula 1 motor racing a thousandth of a second can be the difference between success and failure. So when driver Max Verstappen pulled in for a tyre change at the 2019 Brazilian Grand Prix his Red Bull team had to be on their toes. In the pit, 16 people stand ready, including four tyre swappers with super-powerful pneumatic wheel guns. Pit stops generally take around 2.4 seconds, but this change took a record 1.82 seconds. This video lasts a whole minute but shows the synchronicity and great teamwork in slow motion and from every angle.

FASTEST
FORMULA 1
TYRE CHANGE

BACKWARDS RECORDS

Doing something backwards is a favourite among record breakers. Sometimes skilful, sometimes dangerous and often looking rather silly, our heroes set to their task without fear of neck ache ...

◀ Thunder's Back

http://y2u.be/o4fzSkAgNP4

Although it has since been broken, Thunder Law of the Harlem Globetrotters used to hold the record for the longest-ever basketball shot. And although he has had to give up that crown, he can take solace in an even more incredible achievement: the longest shot facing away from the hoop. His one-handed backward launch propelled the ball 82 feet and 2 inches (25.04 metres) – almost the length of the court and 10 feet (3.04 metres) further than the previous record – for a perfect three-pointer.

◢ Parallel Parking

http://y2u.be/VSp1olKp_f0

Try this manoeuvre when you're faced with a tight parking space at the local supermarket car park. In front of a live audience at the 2015 Performance Car Show, British stunt driver Alastair Moffatt slid a Fiat 500 1.2 Cult into the narrowest of parallel-parking spaces. Moffat's magnificent handbrake turn was made in a standard car with an enhanced steering wheel and pumped-up tyre pressures. Sliding into a space just 3 inches (7.5 centimetres) longer than the car enabled Moffat to reclaim a world record that had been taken from him by a Chinese stunt driver. He bested his rival by half a centimetre.

Get Your Skates On

https://youtu.be/hWGn_v8uO5E

High heels are usually associated with grace and style, but in truth Canadian circus performer Bianca Rossini is not exactly the picture of perfect elegance as she attempts to set a world record for the fastest 328 feet (100 metres) skating backwards in stilettoes. That said, her in-line skates with pink spiky shoes attached do look rather glamorous. Still, the main point here is whether she can stay upright and cross the line in under 30 seconds or fall and fail…

▼ Ramping It Up

http://y2u.be/XUIiffRMfVQ

Ever wondered what skateboarders do for thrills when they grow out of their baggy shorts and elbow pads? Professional skateboarder Rob Dyrdek set 21 different skateboarding records before moving on to be a TV star and all-round entertainer. He broke doughnut-and-banana-eating records on his hit show *Rob & Big*, but once a ramp man … In the parking lot of a theme park, Dyrdek reversed his Chevrolet Sonic off one ramp and flew 89 feet 3¼ inches (27.2 metres) through the air to land cleanly on another. What a guy!

THE WORLD'S LONGEST REVERSE RAMP JUMP

▶ Bowling Backwards

http://y2u.be/ex5iwpBHhdw

YouTube has opened up an opportunity for records to be broken all over the world. You no longer need officials and men in blazers to set an authentic record, just a clear video of your achievement. Step forward the most unlikely looking hero in Andrew Cowen of Illinois, USA. Andrew was determined to throw a 300 score (pretty impossible for us weekend bowlers) – while facing the wrong way. He managed 280 – two more than the official record – and might have reached his 300 if not for that second frame slip-up.

TOTALLY GROSS!

Are you ready to be completely grossed-out? These are some of the yuckiest, flesh-creeping and nauseating clips on the site. And, of course, they are absolutely mesmerizing.

Mayo-nazing

https://youtu.be/_INKqoqDYsk

Michelle Lesco is a competitive eater. She has consumed plates of pasta and hot dogs at top speed, but she may have met her match in mayonnaise. The challenge is to spoon as much of it as possible into your mouth in three minutes. Somehow she downs three large jars and is well on her way through the fourth when the whistle blows. The record stands at 1.8 pounds (815.5 grams), but Michelle manages to slurp down 5.4 pounds (2448 grams) of the creamy gloop – and seems completely unaffected.

MILK-
SQUIRTING
CHAMPION

▶ Squirt Off

http://y2u.be/H7EPl1N_aN4

It's the ultimate squirting-milk-from-the-eye battle! Please don't try this at home. It hurts and can lead to lasting damage to the eyes. Plus, it's altogether a pretty repulsive thing to do. That said, have a look at these two heroes squirting it out for the record. The trick, apparently, is to snort milk up your nose, close your mouth, block your nostrils and build up the pressure in the nose. The milk has nowhere else to go but to escape through a duct in the eyes. Yuk!

MOST COCKROACHES HELD IN THE MOUTH

▼ Cockroach Challenge

http://y2u.be/jtXXWz-iKKQ

Even if celebrity reality-TV shows have made you rather blasé about the eating of creepy crawlies, this record by Travis Fessler of Florence, Kentucky, still leaves an uneasy taste in the mouth. Fessler takes on the world record for putting the most Madagascar Hissing Cockroaches in his mouth. It's enough that he can bear to pick up one of the critters let alone have room to stuff 11 roaches into his mouth at the same time. Animal lovers can relax: all 11 reappear, looking healthy and as disgusting as ever.

MOST SLIME EVER IN ONE PLACE

◤ Sticky Situation

http://y2u.be/IIyEtN8qLmM

Twelve-year-old Madison Greenspan is one self-motivated pre-teen. The youngster, from Connecticut, USA, has been making and selling her Maddie Rae's Slime Glue since she was 10 years old. In November 2017, she found the perfect way to promote it. With the help of hundreds of children and a whole lot of goo, Madison Greenspan broke the Guinness World Record for the largest amount of slime. The children filled a pool with more than 13,000 lbs (5,900 kg) of ooze at the Javits Convention Center, New York City. And naturally enough, they all wanted to wade through the record-breaking gunk.

MULTIPLE RECORD HOLDERS

For some people, breaking one mention in the record books is just not enough. One sniff of glory has them searching for more.

It's a Wrap

https://youtu.be/HZlKyEG8TFk

Don't worry, if you're trying to take the record for the fastest time to wrap someone in cling film or saran wrap, the person you're wrapping will still be able to breathe, because fortunately you only have to cover them from the neck down. David Rush, who loves breaking obscure records, has his wife step in to be his mannequin. Admittedly, she doesn't look that happy about it, and although it does take him 12 attempts and around 1,000 feet (over 300 metres) of plastic, he gets it in the end – to Mrs Rush's great relief!

◄ Joe of all Trades

http://y2u.be/viluI1gCm64

Joe Alexander from Hamburg, Germany, likes a record or two. Well, 10 at the last count. Joe doesn't seem fussy as long as they are records. Among his successes are smashing concrete tiles while holding an egg in his hand, catching marshmallows with chopsticks, and trapping harpoons underwater. On record-breaking day 2013, the self-styled Adrenalin Master gave us two records for the price of one. First up, he walked across 60 champagne bottles in a row without touching the ground. He then followed that up by catching 16 darts with his bare hands.

MOST MARSHMALLOWS CAUGHT WITH CHOPSTICKS

◢ Mr Olympic

http://y2u.be/OK0k6i2d_jk

"This all started with one little dream as a kid to change the sport of swimming and try to do something nobody has ever done," said US swimmer Michael Phelps. Well, he can tick that one off his to-do list. A gold in the men's 4x100 metres medley relay at the 2016 Rio Olympics took Michael Phelps's medal tally to 28 (23 gold, 3 silver and 2 bronze) – 10 more than the next most decorated Olympian, gymnast Larisa Latynina. Despite the announcement of his retirement after the Rio Games, many believe he could be back for more in 2020.

POP'S MOST SUCCESSFUL MUSICIAN

▲ Houston, We Have a ... Beatle

http://y2u.be/hpvE8kVGeZI

Once a member of the Beatles, Paul McCartney has gone on to become the most successful musician and composer in popular music history. He has a host of sales and radio-play world records, the most Number 1 hits ever, the most frequently covered song in history ('Yesterday' has been sung by over 4,000 artists), the largest paid audience for a solo concert (350,000 people, in 1989 in Brazil) – and, perhaps best of all, he was the first artist to broadcast live to space.

BRILLIANT BUILDINGS

Yes, it's interesting to discover the dates and dimensions of the world's record-breaking buildings, but how much better is it to watch one tilting sideways, or being climbed without ropes?

Head for Heights

http://y2u.be/a2p4BOGXSBw

Do you suffer from vertigo? If so, maybe give this video a miss. Here, a man known only as "Urban Endeavors" takes us up 1,500 feet (475 metres), twice the height of the Eiffel Tower, to the very top of the world's tallest TV tower, in North Dakota, USA. The tower itself is an unexceptional structure, but the journey is nail-biting and breathtaking as our guide climbs without ropes or harness; just gloves and bucketfuls of courage. He even forgoes the "easy way up", climbing the outside of the tower, rather than using the central ladder.

▶ Mesmerizing Moscow

http://y2u.be/FS17yy1rlsw

October 2015 saw the Moscow International "Circle of Light" Festival screen the world's largest projected image, a dazzling 205,582.33 feet^2 (19,099.3 metres^2) video animation, onto the iconic architecture of the Ministry of Defence building in Russia. Thousands of people turned up to become mesmerized by the vivid and vibrant visuals, a display that used 140 powerful Panasonic projectors to illuminate the 50-minute film in HD for all to see. Check it out!

LARGEST PROJECTED IMAGE

▶ A Tilt at the Record

http://y2u.be/UEfeqgXPHPA

Everyone has heard of the Leaning Tower of Pisa, some have heard of the leaning tower of Suurhusen (which leans a further 1.22 degrees). However, as of 2010, there is a new leaning king on the block – the Capital Gate in Abu Dhabi. In contrast to the previous record holders, the Capital Gate was intentionally designed to lean. Despite being one of the tallest buildings in the city at 35 storeys high, it keels as much as 18° westwards – more than four times that of Suurhusen.

▶ Go with the Flow

https://youtu.be/xzDs462Gtz0

The first time it was turned on, local residents called the local paper, because they thought the pipes had burst. In fact, the running costs are so high that it isn't turned on very often and then only for 20 minutes at a time. However, the world's tallest man-made waterfall in action is a quite a sight to behold. The water cascades 354 feet (108 metres) down one face of the Liebian International Building, a 397-foot (121-metre) skyscraper in Guiyang, in southern China's Guizhou Province.

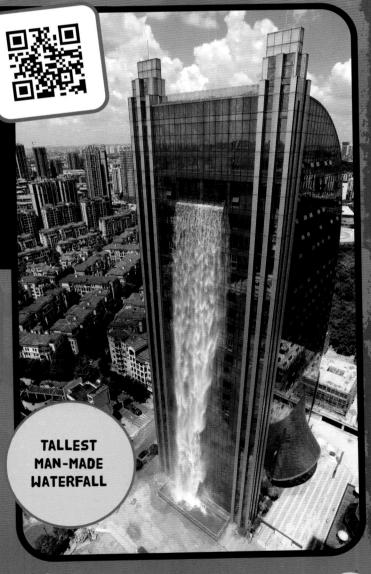

TALLEST MAN-MADE WATERFALL

King of the Castle

http://y2u.be/Qoqx24oXcol

There's no sea and nowhere to lay a towel, but the landlocked German city of Duisburg does have a sandcastle – the biggest sandcastle ever made! Having failed in 2016 after a major castle collapse, the city succeeded the year after with a sandcastle that took 19 sculptors 3 weeks to build and used 4,000 metric tonnes of sand. Their 54.72-foot (16.68-metre) tower, built in a disused coal and steel plant, featured replicas of the Great Sphinx of Giza, Venice's Rialto Bridge, the graveside of Elvis Presley and other global landmarks.

▼ Hit the Roof

http://y2u.be/iD4qsWnjsNU

The Khalifa Tower (Burj Khalifa), a skyscraper in
Dubai, is the highest man-made structure in the
world. Unsurprisingly, it has been a target for BASE
jumpers wanting to set records. Two jumpers
created a world record in 2008 when they illegally
jumped from the 160th floor, but this 2014 "official"
jump surpassed that. Fred Fugen and Vince Reffet
leaped from a platform built above the top of the
building, some 2,716 feet 6 inches (828 metres)
from the ground. They actually did it six times to
make sure the video was impressive!

THE
WORLD'S
TALLEST
BUILDING

SUPER-FAST RECORDS

The best records are those feats we think we can do pretty well ourselves. Just watch these people get dressed, cut hair or throw a Frisbee – and see if you might match them.

Cold Feet

https://youtu.be/-FWFL_6NVd0

Here we have David Rush (he is obsessed with breaking records and you might remember him from page 58) attempting the record for the most socks removed in one minute while blindfolded. Now, there are a number of ways you could do this, but David's set-up is quite simple. It consists of a long line of chairs. There's someone sitting in each chair and… well, you'll see. The terms of the record don't state whether the socks have to be clean or not, but let's hope so.

In the Balance

http://y2u.be/bDFZok9uzdk

Try to balance an egg. It isn't easy, they are just not made for it. It would take most people five minutes to balance one egg. Back in 2003, Brian Spotts helped break the record of most eggs balanced at once with 1,290 eggs. But he was hungry for more records, so he invented the category of fastest time to balance a dozen eggs. Finding his record broken, Brian decided it was time to poach it back – at a shopping mall in Hong Kong.

▼ Plot Twist

http://y2u.be/5x8jgGX3iNM

The Rubik's Cube was invented in 1974 (by Ernő Rubik, of course!) and first went on sale in 1980. With around 350 million cubes sold to date, it is the world's best-selling puzzle game. And a constant world-record challenge. Step forward SeungBeom Cho, the most recent record-breaker. He set his incredible 4.59-second record for the 3 x 3 x 3 cube in a competition in Chicago, USA in 2017. Now, 23-year-old Cho is a highly rated speed-cuber, but his surprise at taking the record is absolutely priceless.

FASTEST RUBIK'S CUBE SOLVER

▶ A Cut Above

http://y2u.be/C1k1kiAd3Bg

There was no time for niceties. No enquiry about holiday destinations. Not even a question about "how would you like your hair today, sir?" Hairdresser Konstantinos Koutoupis from Athens, Greece, had no time to waste if he was going to secure the record for giving the fastest haircut. The rules stated it had to be a "businessman haircut", taking at least half an inch (1.5 centimetres) off all round the head, so Konstantinos couldn't cut corners. With his mirrors cleaned, scissors sharpened and the customer's hair finely combed, Konstantinos had just 50 seconds to deliver…

▼ Sling Shot

http://y2u.be/NRr2zL0PYPA

You wouldn't want to get in the way of a 100-mph (160-km/h) ball thrown by an MLB baseball pitcher or, indeed, face a test cricketer bowling at you at 90 mph (145 km/h). It is, however, Jai Alai – popular in the Basque region, Latin America and the Philippines – that is recognised as the fastest sport in the world. Played on a 175-foot (53-metre) long court with three walls by teams of two players, each with curved baskets that are strapped to their hands, the game sees players consistently catch and throw balls at an incredible 186 mph (300 k/ph).

Speedy Frisbee

http://y2u.be/TO2RQj-L7gg

Simon Lizotte was a Frisbee prodigy. Dubbed "The Wunderkind", Lizotte, from Bremen in Germany, has dominated the German Disc Golf scene for years. He was the 2012 European Champion and is renowned in the game for his power on the drive. He holds the record for the longest disc throw (863.5 feet or 263.2 metres – the length of two-and-a-half football pitches), but here he notches up the fastest throw ever recorded at 89.5 mph (144 km/h).

WORLD'S FASTEST SPORT

SOUND AND VISION

They say it takes all sorts to make a world ... but the record world has the strangest inhabitants of all. Call them weird, call them mad; they call themselves "record breakers"!

Passing the Baton

http://y2u.be/hdflAVImhoU

"There are some difficult parts where the music gets faster, so I have to move my arms more, but I'm getting the hang of it." That's what Matthew Smith told *ITV News* in March 2017 during the Nottingham Symphony Orchestra's rehearsal for Johann Strauss's famous operetta *Die Fledermaus*. However, Matthew knew the piece by heart and, despite it being his first outing with the baton, he was confident of keeping the 75-strong orchestra on track. Which is all pretty impressive when you consider that Matthew is just 11 years old and the youngest ever symphony-orchestra conductor.

YOUNGEST SYMPHONY CONDUCTOR

▶ Fan-tastic Noise

https://youtu.be/JwUuU1M5y_U

Sports fans around the world frequently boast that their team has the loudest support. However, supporters of Kansas University's basketball team, the Jayhawks, can support their claim with an official record. In February 2017, at their Allen Fieldhouse arena, after a game against West Virginia, screaming fans reached a world record level for an indoor crowd of 130.4 decibels. Just to put it in context, live rock music is around 110 dB and a chainsaw can reach 120dB. Now that's what you call getting behind your team. Go, Jayhawks!

Ace of Bass

https://youtu.be/NoChroQIA10

Italian Davide Biale is better known as YouTuber Davie504. His fans, and there are an awful lot of them, are known as 'slappers' – a reference to the bass guitar-playing technique called slapping – and his often-repeated catchphrase is "Slap like now!" In case it's not obvious, Davie is obsessed with the bass. So obsessed that he's built the world's only 36-string bass. It's a strange-looking instrument and clearly quite tricky to handle, but he really can play and he treats us to a virtuoso performance.

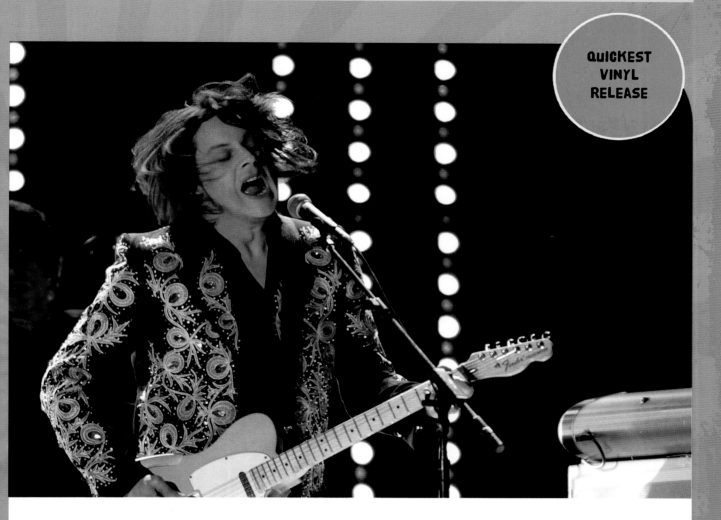

QUICKEST VINYL RELEASE

▲ Press Record

http://y2u.be/xPGK84Yuihc

Vinyl records are hip again and to celebrate Jack White, formerly of The White Stripes, recorded a live version of his song "Lazeretto" and a cover of Elvis Presley's "Power of My Love". While he carried on entertaining the crowd, the masters were rushed off to be pressed and outfitted with sleeves featuring photos from the event. In just under four hours, the single was being bought in stores. Of course, he could have uploaded the songs to YouTube in a matter of moments, but that would have been far too easy!

CRAZY CRITTERS

There's no such thing as a fair fight in the wild. Clawing, biting, stinging and kicking are all allowed. These guys are the best in the business.

Angry Bird

http://y2u.be/6Vqs2ZOOirk

Hailing from the rain forests of Australia and New Guinea, the cassowary has a bony crest on its head capable of knocking down small trees, and dagger-like sharp claws. Growing up to 6 feet (1.82 metres) tall and weighing in at over 130 pounds (59 kilograms), it can reach speeds of 30 mph (48 km/h) – and is capable of kicking with both legs at the same time. They have gutted dogs, slaughtered horses and maimed and even killed humans. The most dangerous bird by far …

Sting in the Tail

http://y2u.be/cWl66-HBnOM

Say hello to the *Androctonus australis* – but don't get too close. The creature's name means "southern man-killer" and, indeed, the fat-tailed scorpion, as it is commonly known, is the deadliest scorpion in the world. Found in the deserts of the Middle East and Africa, the venom of the fat-tailed scorpion causes several human deaths every year. The killer critters aren't huge – they only grow up to 4 inches (10 centimetres) long – but are often found hiding in the brickwork or concrete cracks of houses. So go careful where you put those fingers!

▶ Packing a Punch

http://y2u.be/ti2Uoc1RXuQ

The mantis shrimp is a fabulous creature. A shrimp-sized lobster, it has big bug eyes, comes in dazzling colours and packs the fastest and strongest punch in the animal kingdom. Sometimes referred to as "thumb splitters", their claws are strong enough to split human appendages, and the shrimp has a punch stronger than a .22-calibre pistol. It has even been known to smash the glass of aquariums when riled. Just watch this slow-motion footage of this champion slugger throwing a right hook!

THE SHRIMP THAT PACKS A PUNCH

▶ Iron Jaws

http://y2u.be/akbpHX0Wbvw

The human bite exerts a pressure of around 120 psi (pounds per square inch). It's enough to chomp through an apple or a piece of toffee. Lions and sharks have jaws that are five times as strong – good for tearing raw flesh apart or ripping through a small boat. But the iron jaws of the animal world belong to the Nile crocodile. These beasts can snap at 2,500 psi (and have reached 6,000 psi), twice as much again as the feared shark.

▼ Make it Snappy

https://youtu.be/H2okI6ZszQY

Welcome to the Ant Lab. The trap-jaw ant, known in Latin as *Andontomachus brunneus*, has a super-fast and super-powerful spring-lever jaw. When it attacks, its lower jaw moves at a mind-bending 90 mph (145 km/h), which is roughly the speed of a bullet in the barrel of a gun. One open-and-shut bite takes 312 micro-seconds or one three-thousandth of a second to complete. Just capturing this action in super-slow-motion video is no mean feat, involving both physics and maths. However the question here is, in the battle of the ant versus a finger, who will win?

THE WORLD'S QUICKEST BITE

AMAZING FOOD RECORDS

Groceries – they're not just for eating, you know. You can use them in art, construction, as a pastime – and to break records. Here's some food for thought ...

▶ Pumpkin Pride

http://y2u.be/8eQljtg3tAA

This was the moment the pumpkin world had been waiting for: the first-ever one-ton pumpkin, winning farmer Ron Wallace a $10,000 prize. The historical event happened in 2012 at the All New England Giant Pumpkin Weigh-Off when Wallace's colossal pumpkin was lifted onto the scale by a forklift truck. It topped out at an astounding 2,009 pounds (911 kilograms), beating the record set just the previous day by 165 pounds (75 kilograms) to become the largest fruit ever grown.

Absolutely Ridiculous, Seriously

http://y2u.be/L4Y6VVdk2XY

If the quarter-pounder at your local burger bar is a little insubstantial for you, take a trip to Mallie's Sports Grill & Bar in Detroit, USA. They pride themselves on their "Absolutely Ridiculous Burger", which breaks – and re-breaks – the world record for the largest hamburger commercially available. You'll need to give the restaurant 72 hours' notice and have $2,000 dollars to spare for the 165-pound (75-kilogram) burger. It takes 22 hours to cook and is served with 15 pounds (7 kilograms) of lettuce, 30 pounds (14 kilograms) of bacon, the same amount of tomatoes, and 36 pounds (16 kilograms) of cheese, all on a 50-pound bun (23-kilogram) bun.

THE INCREDIBLE ONE-TON PUMPKIN

THE WORLD'S LARGEST MOSAIC

◀ Coffee Break

http://y2u.be/Kng_LuXl6HI

Albanian artist Saimir Strati's previous work includes mosaic portraits of Leonardo Da Vinci with nails, a galloping horse with toothpicks and singer Michael Jackson with paint brushes. This time he made another mosaic – the largest in the world – with a million coffee beans. Strati says he wants his image of a Brazilian dancer, a Japanese drummer, an American country music singer, a European accordionist and an African drummer to spread the message of: "One world, one family, over a cup of coffee."

▼ Spaghetti Junction

http://y2u.be/v7SgBUq6_qk

Spaghetti Bridge competitions are held in universities around the world as a test for students' knowledge of engineering, physics and design. The bridges are made of only spaghetti and glue and are tested for how much weight they can sustain before they shatter. The Budapest Technical University has a great reputation for setting records and it was their students Miklós Vincze and Csaba Jaró who created Hoverla 5. A beautiful and, as it proved, historic construction, it finally collapsed under a weight of 1,257 pounds (570.3 kilograms).

RECORD-BREAKING SPAGHETTI

SUPER-STRENGTH RECORDS

The human body is a wonderful thing and even if you think you've seen it all, there's always something weird out there that will blow your mind: these record-breakers, for example.

On the Nail

http://y2u.be/W13JvvsKiJM

Extreme-stunts performer "Space Cowboy" calls himself "Australia's most prolific record breaker" – and with good reason. He has over 40 records to his name (which is really Chayne Hultgren), including pulling 411 kilograms by fishhooks in his eye sockets for the furthest distance, the fastest arrow caught blindfolded, and most chainsaw-juggling catches on a unicycle. In 2012, the Cowboy displayed his skills on the TV Show *Australia's Got Talent*. Lying on a bed of over 100 sharp, 8-inch (20-centimetre) nails, he was driven over by 20 motorcycles in 2 minutes.

MONSTER WALNUT-CRUSHER

◄ Busting his Nuts

http://y2u.be/OD1g8fUFdxQ

If you're struggling with the nutcracker again this Christmas, you could try breaking those shells manually. All you need is a little iron-palm training. That's how this martial-arts master gained the strength to set a new world record in Foshan City in southern China's Guangdong Province in 2017. He smashed 302 walnuts in 55 seconds with his bare hands. Before you give it a go, though, bear in mind that kung-fu expert Li Weijun has trained in various kinds of Chinese martial arts for over 27 years.

▶ A Nose-Blowing Champ

http://y2u.be/6LGiq717r9Q

23-year-old Jemal Tkeshelashvili is capable of inflating hot-water bottles to the point of bursting – with his nose! These rubber bottles require ten times more air pressure to inflate than a party balloon, so Jemal needs great lung capacity and the ability to push the air out of his nostrils with incredible force. Here, in 2009, in his home town of Tblisi, Georgia, he blew up and exploded three hot-water bottles in 23 seconds, including one being sat on by a hefty adult.

THE MAN WITH A CHAMPION NOSE

Thigh High

http://y2u.be/TN59gYxa2to

The sport of crushing fruit between your thighs isn't likely to threaten the popularity of football on TV any time soon, but Olga Liaschuk's appearance on British TV show *This Morning* caused quite a stir. Seated on a mat in the studio, and watched over by genial show hosts Phillip Schofield and Holly Willoughby, Olga crushed 3 watermelons between her thighs in just 14 seconds. Ukrainian Olga is also a champion in the perfectly respectable sport of weightlifting, but who wants to watch that when you can see exploding melons?

▼ Miracle Man

https://youtu.be/b-tFgKlqgb0

Mark Felix is 53 years old or, as he prefers to put it, 53 years young, and he's a plasterer by day, strongman by night. He only started entering strongman competitions at 38, but since then he's made up for lost time and qualified for the World's Strongest Man event 14 times. No wonder he's known as 'The Miracle'. Mark trains hard, but also has a handspan of 11 inches (28 centimetres). This probably helps when it comes to the Hercules hold world record, which involves preventing two steel pillars, each weighing 772 pounds (350 kilograms), from toppling over…

Table Manners

http://y2u.be/MC6tgknKPQE

Even among strongmen challenges, some records push the boundaries of the bizarre. Take Georges Christen, a national hero in Luxembourg. In a career spanning over 30 years, Georges has made a name for himself setting records pulling trucks, buses and ships, and even making a huge Ferris wheel turn – all using his teeth. This performance – a repeat of another record-breaking feat – is a little more special. It shows a woman sitting on a table being carried in the air by Georges – yep, you've guessed it – by his teeth! She's seems like a willing participant, but keep an eye on her expression.

HOLDING OUT FOR A HERO

This awesome selection illustrates just how wide-ranging the record-breaking heroes are. Some rely on physical endurance, others on know-how and some are just downright crazy!

◀ Room on the Back

http://y2u.be/6qRzC95YpSE

Plumber Colin Furze's project began in his mum's garden with a normal 125cc scooter, which the ingenious engineer adapted with a home-made aluminium frame, adding 25 seats and extending it to 72 feet (22 metres) – nearly as long as a tennis court. To set the record, Furze had to ride the bike for 328 feet (100 metres), but he actually rode it for over a mile (1.6 kilometres). "When I first got on it, I thought it would never work, and at a slow speed it's almost impossible to keep upright," says Colin, but on Saltby Airfield in Grantham, England, he managed a pretty impressive 35 mph (56 km/h).

▶ Drumroll Please!

https://youtu.be/JrnPBnRegUU?t=568

At the age of two and a half, Siddharth Nagarajan played his first concert and was officially recognized as the youngest ever Indian drummer. Six years later, having been invited onto a National Geographic TV show, he was declared an inborn genius. Now, at the age of 19, Siddharth is a respected percussionist across musical genres and a world-record holder. In 2017 he broke the record for The Most Drumbeats in a Minute Using Drumsticks. His 2,109 beats is equivalent to a staggering 35 beats in a second. Now that's how you "beat" a record.

MOST DRUMBEATS IN A MINUTE

▼ Fast Track

http://y2u.be/H7IwEQGM_Vk

There are many records in this book that are foolish, dangerous or outright idiotic, but this is the only one that is actually criminal. The clip tells the story of Ed Bolian's attempt at the Cannonball Baker Sea to Shining Sea Memorial Trophy Dash, a coast-to-coast drive across the USA and the basis for the movie *The Cannonball Run*. It's a highly illegal race that requires speed limits to be broken all through the journey. Ed reached a top speed of 158.26 mph (255 km/h) and spent 88 per cent of the trip above 80 mph (128 km/h), but he did traverse the country in just 28 hours and 50 minutes.

THE FASTEST DRIVE ACROSS THE USA

Swiss Roll

https://youtu.be/Tez12O9zKZU

The video calls it Swiss ball surfing, but there is no beach and no waves – just a running track and a line of those air-filled exercise (Swiss or Ballast) balls you see in the gym. Aussie Nicholas Smith lines up 26 of these giant balls and precedes to "surf" along the line from one to another, covering a record distance of 255 feet 4.96 inches (77.85 metres). Some may dispute the "surfing" aspect and say that "belly-bouncing" would be a more accurate description, but there can be no denying that it looks like a whole lot of fun.

FURTHEST SWISS BALL "SURF"

How Low Can You Go

http://y2u.be/AaPtiFO-NLc

Tim Storms goes deep for his record. He's no diver, though, as singer Tim holds the world record for reaching the lowest note. Due to his oversized vocal chords, Tim can hit notes so low that only huge animals like elephants can hear them. He has reached a G-7 or 0.189Hz – a note eight octaves below the lowest G on the piano (a whole piano length lower). This gives him another record – the greatest vocal range. He has a full 12 octaves, but Tim has warned he could break records again as his voice continues to get lower as he ages.

TOTALLY DIFFERENT

The record breaker can never stop to ask why. Thankfully, these record setters never questioned putting themselves in harm's way, playing a silly instrument or throwing shaving-foam pies …

Comfort Blanket

http://y2u.be/qK7RYDGj_xk

In February 2016, Mother India's Crochet Queens in Chennai, India, made the largest crochet blanket in the world. How big is it? It's massive! Measuring 120,001 feet² (11,148.5 metres²), the blanket covered an entire football pitch! Creating such a snuggly object took more than 1,000 participants (aged eight to 85), from more than 14 countries, scores of hours to create individual 40 x 40 inch (101.6 x 101.6 centimetres) sections, which were then sewn together to make one ultra-cosy blanket. After the record was verified, the blanket was deconstructed and the sections were donated to local charities.

WORLD'S LARGEST CROCHET BLANKET

▼ Splat's the way to do it!

http://y2u.be/sKOqUJfcUfw

And you think flinging foam pies is just clowns playing around? Listen, there are rules to this sport. The plates must be filled with shaving foam, which has to have a peak, and the flinger must be five feet (1.5 metres) away from the victim. And so to the Kidtropolis show in London in 2017, where "Captain Calamity" and "Colonel Custard" (probably not their real names) are on their fourth attempt at the record for the most shaving-foam pies flung in someone's face in one minute. They have already equalled the record but, if they are going to better it, they need to keep their eyes on the pies…

MOST "PIES" THROWN IN FACE

◀ Raw Geometry

http://y2u.be/C7XY-HvNWas

In the summer of 2016, sushi mosaics were trending on Instagram. Hundreds of pictures showed sushi squares, artistically arranged in colourful geometric patterns. It is a quintessentially Japanese art form – they are exquisite, delicate and precise – so, naturally, the world record for the largest sushi mosaic was set in... Norway, and was created by a chef who runs a sushi bar in Sweden. The mosaic, displayed at the Aspmyra Stadion, in Bode, Norway, measured an incredible 608 square feet (56.50 square metres) and included almost 1,800 pounds (800 kilograms) of salmon, around 900 pounds (400 kilograms) of rice, 44 gallons (200 litres) of rice vinegar, 1,060 pounds (480 kilograms) of cucumber and 22 pounds (10 kilograms) of chives.

WORLD'S LARGEST SUSHI MOSAIC

▼ What a Reaction

https://youtu.be/XXn4fP3CnJg

Elephant's toothpaste is the name given to foam that you can make by mixing the chemical hydrogen peroxide, warm water and a catalyst like yeast or, in this case, potassium iodide. Nick Uhas and the V.Squad have a history of conducting this experiment on a grand scale and here they go for the world record. There's a lot of preparation, some neat DIY and some interesting science involved – and the results are truly spectacular. However, for a number of reasons (see what happens to fellow YouTuber David Dobrik's Los Angeles house) remember not to try this at home!

ELEPHANT'S TOOTHPASTE EXPLOSION

77

COOL CAT RECORDS

There is plenty of kitten action and a lot of celebrity cats on YouTube, but not many make the record books. Here's a select few who are on the road to purr-fection.

Top Cat

https://youtu.be/uTYIwCmdmmk

Meet Nala. She's a Siamese/tabby cross and she's the Kim Kardashian of cats. She holds the world record for the most Instagram followers – 4.3 million and rising – and is officially the most famous cat on the Internet (Grumpy Cat, the previous record-holder, sadly passed away in 2019). Nala is undeniably extremely cute and earns a very good living as an influencer. Her owners are reluctant to reveal exactly how much she makes a year, but it's enough to have bought them not just one, but two, houses.

Toe Business

https://youtu.be/7w86n5pmO1Q

While most cats have 18 toes – five on their front paws and four on their back ones – polydactyl cats have extra digits. Polydactyly is an abnormality that is passed from generation to generation. It has no ill effects, in fact their big paws often make them look extra cute and they have super climbing and hunting skills. So meet Paws, a Minnesota cat who ties for a record number of toes. She has 28 toes, three extra on each forepaw and one extra on each back paw. All together now… Awwww!

▶ Cool Cat

http://y2u.be/eCG-wInJJK0

Cats are well known for having great balance. It's pretty useful for traversing garden fences or catching birds. Boomer, however, is far too cool for that kind of nonsense. The Bengali cat hangs out in Australia and likes nothing better than riding his skateboard. Here is Boomer, in October 2017, breaking his own record (13 people) for the longest human tunnel travelled through by a skateboarding cat. He propels himself through 20 pairs of legs – and still acts like it's really no big deal. He's obviously saving the high fives for his first 360 flip.

MOST TALENTED SKATE-BOARDING CAT

▶ Fat Cat

http://y2u.be/7dVn7KNP0co

Garfield is one of the great cartoon cats, right up there with Tom, Top Cat and Sylvester. Now, there is a real-life Garfield, who shared some of his animated namesake's gargantuan appetite and indolence. Garfield was brought to an animal rescue in Long Island, New York, after his owner passed away, and he shocked the volunteers with his obesity. He tipped the scales at 40 pounds (18 kilograms) – an average cat weighs around 10 pounds (4.5 kilograms) – and earned the distinction of being the fattest cat in the world.

THE WORLD'S FATTEST CAT

◣ Big Big Cat

http://y2u.be/cNJVI0e6Zhw

There are cats, big cats and then there are ligers. Ligers are the offspring of a male lion and a tigress – huge animals that do not exist in the wild and are only bred in captivity. Hercules, who usually lives at the Myrtle Beach Safari wildlife preserve in South Carolina, is the biggest of them all. He is 6 feet (1.82 metres) tall, 12 feet (3.65 metres) long and weighs 900 pounds (408 kilograms) – as big as his parents combined. He may look a handful, but his keepers say he's a real pussycat.

THE WORLD'S LARGEST LIGER

CRAZY CROWD RECORDS

Whoever said "Three's a crowd" wasn't in the record-breaking business. To register in the record books, you need great organization, silly costumes and people in their thousands ...

▼ Who You Gonna Call?

http://y2u.be/dqQCj7WKNgk

"Ghostbusters of the world, gear up!" went the call to arms from Paul Feig, director of the 2016 version of the 1984 supernatural horror-comedy classic. The fans responded and 263 people got their ghost on – dressed up as the film's famous "no-ghost" logo – and gathered at Singapore's Marina Bay Sands to celebrate the launch of the all-female reboot of the *Ghostbusters* film. Star of the movie Melissa McCarthy was also in attendance and in high spirits as the assembly claimed the title of "Largest gathering of people dressed as ghosts at a single venue".

Follow the Leader

http://y2u.be/yg17h5H9YUM

The record for the most people singing in a round was previously held by the Dublin Google office, where 3,798 employees sang Pharell William's "Happy". The new record could not be more different, as to achieve it a choir of 4,166 people in Turkmenistan sang a song penned by the president. The performance of "Forward Only Forward, My Dear Country Turkmenistan" featured a big-screen video of President Berdimuhamedow himself playing a synthesizer and singing along with his people. The song was performed inside a giant yurt measuring 115 feet (35m) in height and 230 feet (70m) in diameter. Not exactly "Happy", but a record is a record.

WORLD'S LARGEST GHOST GATHERING

◀ Bearly Believable

https://youtu.be/SZAZg86qDpk

It's nine minutes into the game, Christian Djoos scores and the ice is flooded with thousands of assorted soft toys. Christian plays for the Hershey Bears American professional ice hockey team based in Pennsylvania, a club famous for its annual teddy bear toss. When the puck crosses the line for the first time in the game, spectators hurl teddies into the arena. It takes about 15 minutes to sweep them all up, but when the count is done 45,650 bears have been thrown and it's a world record. It's quite a spectacle, but you'll be pleased to hear that all the toys were subsequently donated to children's charities.

▶ Flying the Flag

http://y2u.be/GwhtFvUShto

India's rivalry with Pakistan is often hostile but, in December 2014, the stakes were raised when India stole the world record for the largest human flag from their neighbours. Over 50,000 volunteers began gathering at 5.00am in the YMCA ground in Chennai, but it wasn't until noon that they were in position to form the tri-colour flag. Pakistan's previous record was just short of 29,000 – they've probably already started working on recapturing the title.

▼ Ever So Elfish

http://y2u.be/lu8dsjoW5-o

Nearly two thousand Santa's little helpers, aged between nine and 15, put on red, green and white hats, matching T-shirts and pointy plastic elf ears, and formed up outside a shopping mall in Bangkok. Those participating were required to stand still for 10 minutes with their elf ears and hats on. Some didn't make it and others were disqualified for not putting on their elf ears, but 1,792 correctly attired and standing still were enough to set a new record.

RECORD-
BREAKING
NUMBER OF
ELVES

RECORD-BREAKING DOGS

It's dog beat dog in the competition for canine records. You'll love these proud pooches as they show off their record-breaking skills.

THE UGLIEST DOG IN THE WORLD

◀ Ugly Mutt

http://y2u.be/7AkYSGllKTk

Two-year-old Peanut, a mutt who is suspected of being a Chihuahua/Shitzu mix, doesn't have a lot going for him. He was seriously burned as a puppy and lived in an animal shelter for nine months before he found a home. On the looks side, he has matted hair, protruding teeth and looks as much rodent as canine. However, Peanut found fame in California in 2014. In a hotly contested competition, he swept the floor with the other hideous hounds and was crowned the World's Ugliest Dog.

▶ Puppy Love

https://youtu.be/HqG_AW9oVJI

This is Twitty. She's the world's smallest puppy and she can fit in the palm of your hand. When she was born, she weighed a mere 6 ounces (170 grams) and was just 2.5 inches (6.3 centimetres) tall. Chihuahua Twitty claimed the smallest puppy title from Milly, who still holds the record for being the smallest dog in the world. When she's older, perhaps Twitty can shape up to Milly for that record. It's OK, though, because Milly is Twitty's aunt, so if that happens at least the record will stay in the tiny family.

BIGGEST DOG IN THE WORLD

Got this Licked

http://y2u.be/-jsMpxIXaTY

Mochi, or 'Mo' to his friends, is an adorable eight-year-old St Bernard from Sioux Falls, South Dakota. While many dogs like a good slobber, Mo has an advantage – he officially has the longest tongue (on a dog) in the world, with his licker measuring a whopping 7.31 inches (18.58 centimetres). That makes Mo rather good at both licking his own face and cleaning out the peanut-butter jar. Although his owner does have a job mopping up the excessive slobber, she can't help but admit that his loveable personality and charm make it all worthwhile.

▲ Dog Has His Day

http://y2u.be/29NPJDf2qto

As the runt of the litter, nobody expected Freddy to reach any great height. Now five years old, the Great Dane has been crowned the tallest dog in the world. This big, friendly giant measures 41 inches (104.14 centimetres) from his paws to his shoulders, and stands 7 feet and 6 inches (2.29 metres) when on his hind legs. A resident of Leigh-on-Sea in Essex, UK, Freddy is one hungry hound and scoffs down 1 kilogram of minced beef, 250 grams of steak and about 300 grams of liver every day, although he also has a penchant for chicken, peanut butter – and sofas!

THE WORLD'S SMALLEST DOG

▲ Pocket-Sized Pooch

http://y2u.be/fTEIdAyYkac

Like many dogs, Heaven Sent Brandy, the Chihuahua from Florida, USA, is not allowed on the furniture. In her case, it's just because if she jumps off, she'd break a bone. Measuring just 6 inches (15.2 centimetres) from tail to nose, the adorable four-year-old is no bigger than a can of cola and is the world's smallest dog in terms of length. She's a nervous little creature – but who can blame her, when every hulking great human in sight wants to cuddle her?

ENDURING PASSION

Breaking records can require years of grooming, hundreds of hours of practice, meticulous arrangement or serious organization skills. And some just happen in an instance of pure chance.

▶ The Uber

http://y2u.be/YR6Wh2Zy9jE

Uber driver Anthony struck lucky – or possibly unlucky – when he picked up Jimmy Donaldson in North Carolina. For Jimmy Donaldson is also Mr Beast, a YouTuber famous for such jinks as counting to 100,000 and tipping pizza-delivery guys $10,000. Mr Beast was looking for a ride to California on the west coast – a mere 2,256 miles (3,630 kilometres) away. Once Anthony had checked with his wife and called in sick at work, the longest Uber trip ever was on – and it was going to cost a beastly $5,500.

LONGEST UBER JOURNEY EVER

▼ Heavy Metal

http://y2u.be/5UrG-hY8kUc

Frenchman Michel Lotito is honoured with having the strangest recorded diet and it is fair to say that he didn't earn the nickname "Monsieur Mangetout" without tucking into a few odd items. As a child, Lotito suffered from pica, a compulsive disorder in which people eat non-food items. Developing his affliction into an act, he went on to devour beds, television sets, bicycles and shopping carts. His *pièce de résistance* was a Cessna 150 airplane, which took him two years to consume. Lotito died of natural causes in 2007, having partaken of almost nine tons of metal in his lifetime.

▶ Flippin' Heck

https://youtu.be/gyeorXQfnpA

Felixstowe, a seaside town in eastern England, has many claims to fame. Not only is it the UK's largest shipping container port, but it's also home to Dean Gould, who holds the world record for beer mat flipping. His current record stands at 114 mats flipped and here he attempts two new, flipping-related records, this time involving plastic water bottles as well as coasters. Dean is also very generous with his flipping hints and tips, so if you've got some squares of cardboard handy this is something you could – for once – try at home without serious risk of injury. Just try not to poke your eye out…

FASTEST VIOLINIST IN THE WORLD

▲ On the Fiddle

http://y2u.be/PA_1oS8Ch4U

Record holder Ben Lee is no novelty violinist. He was a child prodigy; a student at the London School of Music; played with the Arctic Monkeys, McFly and others; and eventually formed successful rock violin duo Fuse. In the summer of 2009, Lee suffered damage to his right hand and wrist after being run over by a truck while cycling. To inspire his rehabilitation, his bandmate challenged him to break the world record for fastest violinist. In fact, he went on to break the record five times, on both acoustic and electric violin.

It's Da Bomb!

https://youtu.be/fODeb-XvOBc

Bath bombs are the ultimate in good, clean fun, right? Lob one into your bath and it fizzes madly, colours the water and smells delicious. Gift website VAT19 decided to build the world's biggest bath bomb – around a hundred times bigger than the normal ping-pong or tennis ball-sized one you'd use at home. Watch as they scale up the normal ingredients – corn starch, citric acid, baking soda and dye – and make a 2000-lb (900-kg) bath bomb. It's so big they have to roll it into their "bath" (a swimming pool), but is it worth the effort?

AMAZING ATHLETES

Every sport has its record breakers. These stars, whether from well-known sports like football and swimming, or less well-known, like balloon-batting, have some amazing achievements to crow about!

Aye Aye Skipper

https://youtu.be/kOT19pRZ5rE

A small, flat piece of grey stone bounces along a stretch of open water at top speed – a beautiful, awe-inspiring sight. Scotsman Dougie Isaacs has skipped – or skimmed – a stone further than anybody else in the world. Everyone's had a go at the beach, but to do it well requires surprising physical effort and incredible skill. When Dougie's stone finally stutters and sinks, it has travelled an astonishing 399.6 feet (121.8 metres), which is the world distance record for stone skipping.

▼ Up in the Air

http://y2u.be/dOzzQmMsN2Q

"I know it's silly and kind of dumb, but... I'm pretty proud of myself." This video is like a seven-minute version of *Rocky* – a story of determination, hard work and following your dream. Buzzfeed employees Liem, Katelyn and Jeremy had a chance to write their names in the history books by keeping three balloons in the air for a minimum of 5 minutes and 35 seconds. Easy? Apparently not, but Jeremy is not one to give up easily. Surely, with a little training, he can break that record! This is his story. And good fun it is too.

BEST BALLOON BATTERS

► Lucky Punt

http://y2u.be/ut9dfvgurHY

Seeing a goalkeeper score is one of football's great collector's items. When the ball was passed back from the kick-off to English team Stoke City's Bosnia and Herzegovina international goalkeeper Asmir Begovic, his intention wasn't to join the small band of keeper-scorers. However, with just 13 seconds left on the clock, his up-field punt caught the wind and bounced over opposite number Artur Boruc into the Southampton team's net. It was the sixth-fastest goal in Premier League history but, more importantly, at 301 feet (91.9 metres), it was the longest in competitive football anywhere in the world.

▼ Jump at the Chance

http://y2u.be/kPZvtlDLjpl

This is an unofficial world record, but there appears no reason to doubt it – and it is exceptional. It features Kevin Bania, a CrossFit athlete (CrossFit is a sport featuring weightlifting, sprinting and jumping exercises). Bania attempts a record standing box jump, which involves jumping onto a box or level surface. From a standing start, he leaps from the floor to a platform 5 feet 4.5 inches (1.63 metres) high. Bania himself stands 5 feet 10 inches (1.78 metres) tall, so he is within six inches (15 centimetres) of jumping his own height.

THE MAN WHO JUMPS ALMOST AS HIGH AS HIMSELF

WILD SPORTS

Terrified by the high board at the pool? Dizzy on the top storey of the multi-storey car park? Then perhaps you should just sit down and watch some people who know no fear ...

▼ New Ball Game

http://y2u.be/NehU-6NCBco

Zorbing is the sport of rolling down a hill in the kind of plastic sphere given to bored hamsters. Protected by a pocket of air between them and the edges of the ball, the participants can thrust the ball forward but have limited control over the direction. Miguel Ferrero from Spain, nicknamed "The Adventurer", was encased in a Zorb ball and threw himself down a ski run at La Molina in the Pyrenees. He reached a record speed of 31.2mph (50.2km/h).

THE FASTEST ZORBING ON RECORD

◄ Extreme Swimming

http://y2u.be/IJY8VgmvXHc

Diana Nyad became the first person to swim the 100 miles (160 kilometres) from Cuba to Florida without a protective shark cage. Braving rough seas, the fear of shark attack, vomiting from salt-water intake and wearing a heavy suit to withstand jellyfish stings, Diana succeeded on her fifth attempt over 35 years – her fourth since turning 60.

Snow Business

http://y2u.be/f0mTTmOuvUQ

France's Edmond Plawczyk had waited a long time to reclaim his snowboarding speed record. He had originally set the world record in 1997, but that was broken in 1999. April 2015 was payback time as Edmond donned his strange-looking red winged suit and aerodynamic helmet at the top of the slopes of the famous Chabrières piste in the French Alps. He was soon flying down the 4,600-foot (1,400-metre) course, which at one point measured a gradient of 98 per cent, to realise his ambition and a new record speed of 126.309 mph (203.275 km/h). Sweet.

▼ Water Wall

https://youtu.be/-ucBfEDVJbA

Woah! This wave is bigger than a house. In fact, this wave is bigger than a 12-story block of flats and Briton Tom Butler is riding it. The location is Praia do Norte beach, near the fishing village of Nazaré in Portugal. It's a place which is known for its massive swells, but this one was really massive. In fact, observers estimated the height of this particular wave as more than 100 feet (30.5 metres) high. It's certainly pretty intimidating – scary even – and afterwards Tom admitted that surfing it was like "running away from a raging bull".

THE LARGEST WAVE EVER SURFED

TRULY REMARKABLE

It's a wonderful record-breaking world and YouTube contributors across the globe are out filming every remarkable event and achievement.

Suds and Scrubs

http://y2u.be/b4zLZB4cPBU

In a state whose unofficial motto is "Go Big or Go Home!", Buc-ee's Car Wash in the town of Katy has stepped up to the plate. Buc-ee's were a chain of convenience stores known for Beaver Nuggets, Texas-themed tourist trinkets and immaculate bathrooms, but now they have a new boast. The Katy store has the longest car-wash conveyor belt. Measuring 255 feet (77.72 metres) long with 25 foam brushes and 17 blowers, it takes 5 minutes for a dirty car to enter at one end and emerge clean at the exit.

▼ Pop-Up Painting

http://y2u.be/BV4Vj8Je3bQ

In June 2014, world-famous Chinese artist Yang Yongchun unveiled a special piece of art. Named *Rhythms of Youth*, it depicted the impressive architectural landscape of Nanjing and the Yangtze River that runs through it. Not only was it the largest and longest street painting in the world, measuring an astonishing 1,200 feet (365 metres) long and covering 28,000 sq. feet (2,600 sq. metres), but it was also an anamorphic painting – created in a distorted manner to make it appear three-dimensional.

THE LONGEST STREET PAINTING

▶ A Fine Line

http://y2u.be/y4VJssQv_Qw

Domino-line topples – you either love them or you hate them. If you fall into the latter category, best move along. For the rest of us, there is something hypnotic and satisfying about dominoes falling one by one. This is a single line, so no effects, no dominoes lifted by cranes or toppled by balls – just straightforward domino action. And, after spending two days putting 15,524 multi-coloured dominoes in line and initiating a 5-minute toppling sequence, professional domino artist Lily Hevesh earned the record for the longest domino line ever. Exquisite.

LONGEST LINE OF DOMINOES EVER TOPPLED

▼ Mummy Mia

https://youtu.be/60IjsBZ-LtI

This is one of those that falls into the category of mind-bendingly pointless but nonetheless makes your jaw drop. Here we have a reproduction of the famous death mask of the boy pharaoh Tutankhamun, but in black and white rather than the familiar blue and gold. That's because it's made from cups of coffee – a staggering 7,260 of them. It also took 143 pounds (65 kilograms) of coffee, 1,760 pints (1,000 litres) of milk, 5,279 pints (3,000 litres) of water and 12 hours to set the record. But was it de-coffin-ated…?

▼ A Real Blast

http://y2u.be/iFC8hFci2kI

The best firework displays always keep something special back for the grand finale of the show. The display for the Feast of St Catherine in Zurrieq, Malta, certainly didn't disappoint. The crowds that had gathered at one of the island's biggest festivals witnessed the spectacle of the world's single biggest firework. The rocket, called the *ballun tal-blalen* (which loosely translates as "balloon of balls"), exploded from a 10-foot-wide (3-metre) shell weighing 570 pounds (260 kilograms), launching a chain reaction that saw the whole sky covered in chrysanthemum-pattern lights. Enjoy – it may not last long, but the brief effect is completely dazzling.

◀ Balloon Loon

https://youtu.be/giKqzGGcq8E

The unwritten law of record breaking is that if it's dangerous enough, someone will try it. Here's 26-year-old Remi Ouvrard who took to the skies over Chatellerault, western France, in a balloon piloted by his father. Rather than standing in the basket as normal, Remi sat on a metal chair on top of the inflated canvas sphere and as it rose more than 1000 metres (3,280 feet) above sea level, the daredevil stood up and danced. There wasn't even a record to break in this category but, thanks to Remi, there is now!

HIGHEST ALTITUDE SAT ON TOP OF A BALLOON

IT TAKES ALL SORTS

Isn't it a wonderful record-breaking world when a twerking champion and an underwear-wearer can share a page with the world's greatest footballing cyclist?

▼ Hard Twerk

http://y2u.be/otZmEyIDGsY

After Miley Cyrus's twerking at the 2013 MTV Video Music Awards, New Orleans rapper Big Freedia set about reclaiming the dance. The self-proclaimed Queen of Bounce claimed twerking had been started by the "bounce" dance scene of New Orleans. So, in her home town, Big Freedia – the stage name of Freddie Ross – cued her hit "Duffy", and led a world record 410 dancers, ranging from age 8 to 80, as they shook their rumps for two continuous minutes.

CHAMPION TWERKING IN NEW ORLEANS

▼ Everybody Freeze!

http://y2u.be/BrfN_o91Igg

Autumn 2016 and a new craze was sweeping the Internet: the Mannequin Challenge. Across numerous platforms, people shared videos of groups acting as if they had been frozen in time. Perhaps the most famous video came from the White House and featured Bruce Springsteen, Tom Hanks, Diana Ross and others (you can view it on YouTube). Of course, competition for the biggest Mannequin Challenge was soon on, with pride of place going to this magnificent effort by 55,000 spectators, players, staff and paramedics at a Cape Town sevens rugby tournament in South Africa's Cape Town Stadium.

WORLD'S LARGEST MANNEQUIN CHALLENGE

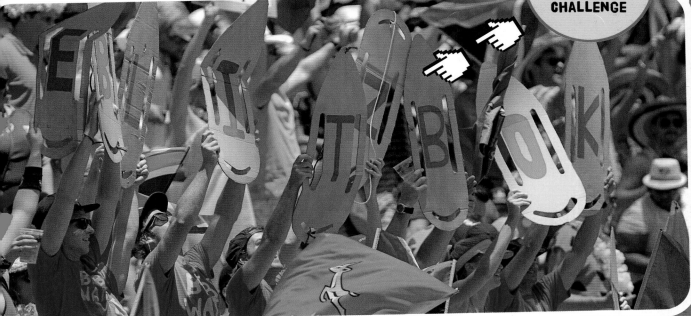

On My Head!

http://y2u.be/joA086aXDlk

As a Nigerian footballer in Cambodia, the possibility existed that Harrison Chinedu might have got overlooked by the national team's coaches. But Harrison was hard to miss when, kitted out in the national strip, he rode a bicycle from a beach outside Nigeria's capital Lagos all the way into the city to the national stadium. Oh, did I forget to say that he did the whole 64 miles (103 kilometres) balancing a football on his head? Six months earlier, his record walk with a ball on his head (28.84 miles/48.04 kilometres) had been quickly broken, so this time he's hoping he's in the record books to stay.

Over and Out

https://youtu.be/YJsKFEWT_E0

Xie Desheng is a martial arts champion and he's pretty handy with a pair of sticks connected by a short chain otherwise known as nunchucks. He moves along a line of candles with – it's the only way to describe it – ninja-like precision, extinguishing flame after flame as he goes. It's mesmerising and he puts out 52 candles in just 60 seconds, which why he's the world record-holder at this discipline. Incidentally, in some countries nunchucks are considered offensive weapons and it's illegal to own or to use them – you have been warned…

▼ Pulling Faces

http://y2u.be/Sp4M2GcnRlE

Tang Shuquan of Chengdu City, China, spends a lot of time hoping the wind doesn't change direction and he stays "like that". Named the King of Deformed Faces, Tang spent 10 years working on being able to contort his face into the ugliest shapes possible. After winning the world record for gurning, Tang, who has the extraordinary ability of biting his own nose, even challenged all-comers – offering a £10,000 prize to anyone who can match his face-stretching skills.

THE GuRNING WORLD CHAMPION

MAD MOVIE RECORDS

Roll the credits! From Bollywood to Hollywood, the glamorous and exciting world of the movies lists the famous and the not so famous in its annals of achievement.

AN EXPENSIVE RECORD BREAKER

◀ Titanic Record

http://y2u.be/2e-eXJ6HgkQ

The 1997 film *Titanic* starring Leonardo DiCaprio and Kate Winslet was, at the time, the most expensive film ever made. It was worth it. *Titanic* became the most successful film ever in terms of box-office and critical success. It has the most Oscar nominations (14, tied with *All About Eve*) and the most Oscar Awards (11, tied with *Ben-Hur*) and is the second-highest-grossing film ever (*Avatar* is first), having taken over 2.2 billion dollars at the box office.

A Dress to Impress

http://y2u.be/RPW3kavkoFQ

On 19 May 1962, during the 45th-birthday celebrations for President John F. Kennedy, actress Marilyn Monroe sashayed onto the stage at Madison Square Garden, took off her fur coat and famously sang "Happy Birthday, Mr President". Under that fur coat Marilyn was wearing a sheer, sequinned dress so tight that she had to be sewed into it. It was an era-defining moment. Fast-forward 54 years and that same dress is under the hammer at auction. It was bought by Ripley's Believe It or Not for an incredible $4.8 million (£3.7 million), making it the most expensive dress ever.

▲ Minute Movie

http://y2u.be/oSCX78-8-q0

Like many great movies, *A Boy and His Atom* has a heart-warming friendship at its centre and – no spoilers here – a moving ending. It has been watched over 6 million times since it was uploaded in 2013, which is particularly astounding as it can't really be seen by the human eye. IBM researchers used a scanning, tunnelling microscope to move thousands of carbon-monoxide molecules (two atoms stacked on top of each other) to make a film so small it can be seen only when you magnify it 100 million times. It's the world's smallest stop-motion movie.

Extra Special

http://y2u.be/miuzO4yI0V4

Acclaimed director Richard Attenborough faced a real challenge when filming *Gandhi* on location in India in 1980. He was determined to re-create the great man's life as accurately as possible and had to film a funeral scene in which a million people had lined the route. Attenborough chose to film on the thirty-third anniversary of Gandhi's funeral and managed to recruit around 300,000 volunteers and actors – the most extras ever to appear in a feature film.

The Car's the Star

https://youtu.be/l5qKCpqNBwo

If anything qualifies as a genuine movie icon it's this 1968 Ford Mustang GT, as driven at break-neck speed through the streets of San Francisco by Steve McQueen in the famous film, *Bullitt*. Having been used as a family runaround, the car had been sitting in a garage for over 30 years, but in early 2020 it came up for auction. Normally this particular model in this sort of condition would be worth about $25,000, but it went for a gobsmacking $3.74 million.

TRANSPORT RECORDS

This collection of the bizarre, brilliant, marvellous and downright silly means of transport would get some strange looks down the High Street.

Life in the Fast Lane

https://youtu.be/CTgLnUgzZYk

It's got a bar of Turkish Delight as a gear stick, the indicators are flashing flower pots and the speedometer is a mantelpiece clock. It's quite a sight and people certainly stare when this sofa on wheels takes to the road. Mind you, the glances aren't always admiring – but perhaps that's the less-than-tasteful furry fake leopard skin it's covered in. According to that mantelpiece clock, it does 90 mph (145 km/h), which makes it the fastest sofa in the world!

THE WORLD'S FASTEST DODGEM

▼ All the Fun of the Fair

http://y2u.be/fGr0oifJMEI

Shouty Colin Furze (watch his fun videos) is a modern-day, record-breaking hero. He's the creator of the world's longest motorbike, the world's fastest pram, the world's fastest toilet and numerous other hilarious and impressive inventions and modifications. His latest project is the world's fastest fairground dodgem car, to be driven by the Stig from TV's *Top Gear* series. Adding a 600-cc Honda motorbike engine will help raise the dodgem's normal speed of 5 mph (8 km/h), but can it make the required 100 mph (160 km/h)? Just hope there's nothing coming in the opposite direction!

One-Wheeled Wonder

http://y2u.be/Jzeq7FWl3Dg

The idea behind the monowheel is simple: build a big enough wheel and you can fit a person inside. Motorized monowheels have been around since the 1930s, but issues with balance, steering and visibility make them dangerous to ride. Kevin Scott built his monowheel, *War Horse*, from a 200cc go-kart engine. It has a diameter of 59 inches (1.5 metres) and the only way to change direction is by leaning. Nevertheless, in September 2016, in Yorkshire, England, Kev rode along an airstrip and back, clocking up a record speed of 61 mph (98.5 km/h).

◢ Poor Man's Porsche

https://youtu.be/OgImEeX8-PI

A casual glance at the race track footage might reveal a sleek silver Porsche 911 elegantly speeding along in slow motion. A closer look, however, will confirm that the Ferdinand GT3 RS is not that. It's actually a bike covered with a sports car chassis that's coated in silver foil – and that isn't slow motion, it's real time (watch to the end to see the moment the real thing speeds by). Austrian artist Hannes Langeder is the creator and "driver" of the Ferdinand, the world's slowest Porsche, and his deadpan presentation makes for an hilarious five-minute super car video.

WORLD'S HEAVIEST WORKING BICYCLE

▲ Heavy Going

http://y2u.be/Zm3ROyV1dhA

You won't see this kind of bike steaming up Alpe D'Huez in the Tour de France, but Frank Dose's extraordinary vehicle is already a winner. The bike, which took him six months to build, broke the record for the heaviest bike in the world, weighing in at over one ton. Despite the fact that it sports 5-foot (1.53-metre) diameter tyres from an industrial fertiliser spreader, a frame made from scrap steel and a beer-crate saddle, Frank still managed to pedal the required 328 feet (100 metres) to earn himself the record.

BIZARRE PEOPLE

The say: "If you've got it, flaunt it." None of these record breakers seems to have any problem flaunting their special features. And, as you will discover, they are pretty special ...

▼ Tongue-Tied

http://y2u.be/h3Ys5aWrbNc

Byron Schlenker always thought his tongue was a real mouthful but never dreamed it could be a record breaker until he helped his daughter, Emily, 14, with a school project. Seeing a picture of an Australian man who claimed to have the world's widest tongue, he began to wonder if his own tongue measured up. Soon he discovered that not only did he have an even wider tongue, but also that Emily had the record female equivalent! Byron's measures a whopping 3 ⅜ inches (8.6 centimetres) across – ¾ inch (2 centimetres) wider than an iPhone 6 – and Emily is not far behind at 2 ⅞ inches (7.3 centimetres).

LARGEST TONGUES IN THE WORLD

◀ The Eyes Have It

The average person's eyelashes measure 1 centimetre (0.39 inches) or so. They do their job of protecting the eye pretty well. Some people apply alluring false eyelashes, which extend their length to around 1.5 centimetres (0.59 inches), but Shanghai-born You Jianxia has eyelashes that reach an incredible 12.4 centimetres (nearly five inches). They hang down the side of her eyes to her mouth like jungle vines or delicate school-gym climbing ropes. You claims her lashes only began to grow after she retired from her high-status finance post and started spending more time in her garden, and she credits the amazing length to being at one with nature.

THE WOMAN WITH THE LONGEST LASHES

▶ That's Nailed It!

Texas-born Ayana Williams's journey to fame began with a simple dare: a friend challenged her to grow her fingernails longer than three inches (7.6 centimetres). More than 20 years later, she still hasn't cut them and each of her nails has grown over 15 inches (40 centimetres) long. In fact, she has a total of nearly 19 feet (5.7 metres) of nail. She admits that having such long nails brings its own problems: she uses a pencil to type on the computer, has to go careful her nails don't get caught in the steering wheel when driving and can't tie her own shoelaces!

Back to Front Boy

It was at a Minecraft conference in 2015 that 14-year-old Maxwell Day revealed his unique skill. Having seen a photo of the record-holder for largest foot rotation, he was soon demonstrating that he could rotate his right foot 157 degrees and turn his left foot round by 143 degrees, easily breaking the previous record of 120 degrees. Maxwell, from Enfield in the UK, asserts that he feels no pain when rotating his feet and he is able to walk with them rotated (although not fast enough to claim that record – yet).

EXTREME EATING

The world of competitive eating is not for the faint-hearted or for those brought up not to shovel down their food. But it is pretty amazing ...

Open Wide

https://youtu.be/_DLCnkUev2k

Do you like burritos? Sure you do. But could you eat one as fast as competitive eater, Leah Shutkever – or Shuteater, as it says on her T-shirt? Leah is a well-known YouTuber, and was featured in the *Battle of the Super Eaters* TV documentary. She's not big. In fact, she's pretty slight, despite the fact she apparently consumes an incredible 10,000 calories on a daily basis. Here she tries to wrap up the world record for speed burrito-eating.

QUICKEST BURRITO CONSUMED

I Scream, You Scream...

https://youtu.be/EaHrWPkWtOU

There was no brain freeze for Miki Sudo when she attended the first ever World Ice Cream Eating Championship at the Indiana State Fair in Indianapolis in 2017. Miki scoffed down 16.5 pints (9.38 litres) of vanilla ice cream in just six minutes. That's equivalent to around 28 large tubs of frozen deliciousness. Miki, of course, has form for this kind of thing. She is currently the top-ranked female competitive eater in the US and holds the records for fastest time to eat 50 Creme Eggs (6 minutes, 15 seconds) and chugging a gallon of milk before sky diving (54.25 seconds).

▶ Sprout About It

http://y2u.be/7Jl8gf2V98U

For many people, Brussels sprouts represent the unacceptable side of Christmas dinner, left on the side when all else has been polished off. Not for Emma Dalton, though. The surprisingly slim 27-year-old competitive eater, who has stuffed back a 5,000-calorie burger in under 10 minutes, has worked her way through the world's biggest helping of sprouts. In one sitting lasting just over half an hour, she scoffed 325 of the mini cabbages – that's almost 7 pounds (3 kilograms) of festive veg. Mind you, not even Emma seems to actually like sprouts, as she coated them in mint sauce, gravy and ketchup to help wash them down.

WORLD RECORD BRUSSELS SPROUTS EATER

▶ Kobayashi — the Master Eater

http://y2u.be/Y5oY5FYULoU

Kobayashi (see page 37) is arguably the world's greatest competitive eater. He has been blowing away his rivals in competitions for 15 years. He has pigged down hot dogs, tacos, satay, noodles and even cow brains, all in world-record time. Here is the master in action on a TV show in 2012, in which he set the record for most Twinkies eaten in a minute. A Twinkie is a "Golden Sponge Cake with Creamy Filling". One is delightful. Two can be sickly. Kobayashi ate 14 ...

THE CHAMPION COMPETITIVE EATER

Blowing Bubbles

http://y2u.be/alBUeRNOaIw

Champion bubble blower Chad Fell of Alabama blew a bubblegum bubble with a diameter of 20 inches (50.8 centimetres) that remained intact for a full five seconds. It was no fluke. Chad takes his skill seriously. He gets through two bags of Dubble Bubble a week in practice and knows his science. He drinks cold water to regulate the temperature in his mouth and chews for 15 minutes to cut down the sugar to aid elasticity before carefully adding air.

▼ Oh, Crumbs

http://y2u.be/OZMMSW4Ackk

Many of the records in this book are impossible for readers to try at home. They are either dangerous, expensive, require specific skills or are just too gross. So here's one you can have a go at yourself. All you need is a chocolate muffin and a camera. Watch the video, study the tactics of Kyle Thomas Moyer of Pennsylvania, USA, who set the record for the fastest time to eat a muffin without using your hands, and prepare your attempt. The target to beat is 28.18 seconds, and remember: no hands!

Appetite for Success

https://youtu.be/YAS8GAm-TMg

Some claim there has been an eating competition at Nathan's Hot Dogs in Coney Island since 1916. That may or may not be true, but since the late 1990s, 20 or so competitors have sat on the raised platform chomping their way through multiple hot dogs and buns in pursuit of the "mustard-yellow belt". For over 10 years, Joey Chestnut has been synonymous with the competition, winning the belt every year except one. Single-handedly, he has taken the 10-minute world record from 58 to a stupendous 74 hot dogs, with this 2018 bread-and-sausage eating display.

▼ Furious —
and Tearful

http://y2u.be/Jky1gDSw0AM

Furious Pete (real name Pete Czerwinski) is a major player in the competitive eating world. He holds six world records, including polishing off 17 bananas in two minutes, wolfing down 15 hamburgers in 10 minutes, guzzling a bottle of olive oil (25 fluid ounces/750 millilitres) in 60 seconds, and tucking away 17 jaffa cakes in 60 seconds. Pete confesses, however, that eating a whole onion in 43 seconds was the toughest of all. Watch his first failed attempt, and you'll see why.

MULTIPLE FOOD-EATING WORLD RECORD HOLDER

NICE MOVES!

These entertaining clips pay homage to the hot-footers who have danced themselves into a pirouetting, head-spinning, pole-leaping, tip-tapping, mascot jiving, record-breaking world.

Lords of the Dance

https://youtu.be/dRE7rU4lk-g

This video is a showcase for Fricska, a Hungarian folk dancing group. Maybe you're not that interested in folk dancing, but it's folk dancing with a modern twist, injected with incredible pace, and it's spectacular. These boys practise hard – they have the blisters to prove it – and among their achievements is the record for the fastest folk dance. However, their hitting and slapping is faster than the human eye can compute, so to verify their record attempt the judges had to watch it back in slow motion, but, yes, these dancers hit and slapped 3937 times in two minutes.

▼ Body Popping

http://y2u.be/yHzpcBuQlpM

Julia Gunthel goes by the stage name Zlata. A 27-year-old Russian living in Germany, she is also known as the Most Flexible Woman on Earth. Watching the way she twists and bends her body around, it is hard to imagine that Julia actually has a spine. Her balloon-bursting act just has to be seen to be believed. She manages to burst three balloons in 12 seconds, using the curve of her back as a press. That just can't be comfortable.

▶ Human Propeller

http://y2u.be/EZfVAxG2-h4

The headspin, a staple power move of breakdancing, is a routine where the dancer's body is rotated while standing on his head. Just watch the poise and strength of 23-year-old Aichi Ono of Japan as it seems he tries to screw his head into the ground. The Human Tornado, or Spinboy as he is also called, spins at a breakneck speed, racking up an incredible 142 rotations in a minute on a TV show in Japan.

RECORD-BREAKING NuMBER OF HEADSPINS

Limbo Queen

http://y2u.be/tqI4NKLhhvU

Shemika Charles is the world-famous Limbo Queen. Ever since setting fire to the Guinness World Record for limbo-ing a mere 8.5 inches (21.5 centimetres) from the floor live on TV in 2010, Ms Charles has travelled the world, showing off her unique talent. In June 2015, however, the Limbo Queen took her skills to a whole new low – and limboed *under a car!* The first world record of its kind and genuinely unbelievable!

In a Spin

http://y2u.be/_U827SJO3Qw

Kinderdijk is famous for its 18th-century windmills – and now for the classic breakdance move that shares the name. More than 70 b-boys from the Netherlands, Italy and France gathered in front of the town's iconic structures to spin on their back and shoulders – a precarious move in the middle of the waterway. Nevertheless, they succeeded in setting a new world record for the number of simultaneous windmills performed in 30 seconds.

THAT'S GOTTA HURT!

"Now that has got to hurt." Sometimes you feel as if you are about to experience the pain yourself as you watch these record breakers undergo self-torture. Of course you aren't. Still, "Ouch!"

Yes He Can

https://youtu.be/l1ztoXgwsj4

They now call him "Can Head", but back when he was just plain Jamie Keeton he was watching a baseball match and happened to place a cold can of cola against his head to cool himself down. Surprisingly, he found the can stuck to his head. Jamie had discovered he had a unique talent – an ability to stick not just cans but any solid object to his head. Is he some kind of mutant? Is it to do with how he sweats on that bald pate? Whatever the science, it has made Jamie a record-breaker. He's managed ten cans at one time and that's going to take some beating.

▼ Bit of a Mouthful

https://youtu.be/E6RWStRqEqk

It's that man again. David Rush (see pages 58 and 64) is going for his 100th world record and this time he's stuffing 100 candles in his mouth. He then has to light them and keep them in place for 30 seconds. That might not seem very long, but time passes slowly when you've turned yourself into a human flare, and they're not tiny birthday cake candles either (which is probably safer, because he's less likely to singe his nasal hair). Can he do it? It's fun seeing him try.

▼ The Flame Game

http://y2u.be/cNuwX0hTFKU

When you take a spoonful of soup and realise slightly too late that it's still too hot for you, that soup is around 85°C. If you're unlucky, your tongue will be blistered for a day or two. Now consider Brad Byers, a man nicknamed the "Human Tool Box" (because he can insert tools through his nasal cavities, but that's another story). Brad trumps your hot soup by more than 20 times as he extinguishes a propane blow torch on his tongue. Incredibly, he's basically licking a 2,000°C flame – what on earth can his tongue be made of?

▶ A Real Buzz!

http://y2u.be/8rlX4APbHTY

You may have heard of bee "beards" but watch this video and you'll see it's more of a bee full-face helmet – there are bees covering his whole face, head and shoulders! Juan Carlos Noguez Ortiz is the hero of the hour. After hanging a tiny cage containing the queen bee from his chin, a colony of 100,000 worker bees is released, huddling around her and settling over the rest of his face. Incredibly, Juan sits it out for 61 minutes as a crowd at Yonge-Dundas Square in Toronto looks on in admiration and bemusement.

MOST TIME SPENT COVERED IN BEES

▲ Heavy Metal

http://y2u.be/Rj7vKStJmtA

A living confusion of tattoo and glistening metal, Elaine Davidson is the world's most-pierced woman. A Brazilian-born nurse, living in Edinburgh, Elaine has 462 studs and rings (192 on her face), which saw her crowned the world's most-pierced woman in 2000. But Elaine didn't stop there – as of March 2012, she had amassed over 9,000 piercings. She never removes the rings and studs, which means she carries around an extra 6.6 pounds (3 kilograms). But you wouldn't miss her in a crowd!

THE WOMAN WITH THE MOST PIERCINGS

THE MOST EXPENSIVE

You'll be surprised at some of the things that turn up in the "most expensive" basket in the YouTube supermarket. Who would expect some scorpion venom next to a masterpiece?

◀ Flight of Fancy

http://y2u.be/s2d_XiJHmdI

If you're taking a flight from New York City to Abu Dhabi, why not travel in style? In fact, why not book a flight on Etihad Airways' Airbus A380? Ask for their luxury suite, "The Residence". At a mere $32,000, it's the world's most expensive flight. The five-star suite comprises an elegantly furnished double bedroom, a lounge with a flat-screen TV and a shower room, and comes complete with a Savoy Hotel trained butler to prepare your bed and ensure your comfort. What's that? You're booked in economy? Oh well, maybe you can wangle an upgrade! This video shows the first lavish leg of the trip

▼ Breaking the Banksy

https://youtu.be/eXKE0nAMmg4

It was the moment that shocked the whole art world. "Girl With Balloon", a famous work by British artist Banksy, had just been sold for over a million pounds. However, as the hammer fell, the painting was sucked into a shredder that had been hidden in its ornate, gilded frame. Banksy later revealed he had secretly built a shredder into the frame years before, in anticipation of this moment. Ironically, the picture was estimated to be worth up to 50 percent more in its shredded state. It might be some time before we witness a faster destruction of a million-pound masterpiece.

THE MOST EXPENSIVE WORK OF ART

◀ Sting in the Tale

http://y2u.be/RCcY0n_7DDs

The list of the most expensive liquids on earth is fascinating: perfume, champagne and human blood are all predictably on the list; there are some surprises like maple syrup and nasal spray; and no computer user would be surprised to see printer ink near the top at around $8,000 a gallon. Just be thankful, then, that you don't need too much scorpion venom (used in anti-cancer drugs). Scorpions are difficult and dangerous to obtain and milk (see the video!) and their venom fetches an amazing $40 million a gallon.

Gold Caller

https://youtu.be/gl62BSjp7Vo

Plated in 24-carat gold, studded with 137 diamonds and with an intricate watch mechanism on the back, this is no ordinary iPhone 11 Pro. Watch as YouTuber Marques Brownlee unboxes the most expensive iPhone in the world. It's available in a limited edition of just one and costs $100,000, so you'll need to save up, but console yourself with the fact that the ticking from the watch would probably be really annoying when you're making a call and all that gold makes it far too heavy to carry around with you…

▲ It's Not About the Money

http://y2u.be/hmXECFLAGNM

THE MOST EXPENSIVE FOOTBALL PLAYER

'It isn't about the money,' insisted Brazilian soccer star Neymar Jr on joining Paris Saint Germain in August 2017. Journalists, however, spoke of little else when PSG activated his $263-million release clause from Barcelona – as the BBC commentator remarked, for that money they could have bought three Boeing 737-700 passenger planes or enough spaghetti to cover the whole of Barcelona. And, they weren't finished there. Neymar's five-year contract is reportedly worth around $45 million a year before tax, making him the highest-paid player in the history of the sport. Is he worth it? This clip shows why PSG had every reason to be pleased with their purchase…

A LONG WAY DOWN

Some people just have no respect for the laws of gravity. It might have kept sensible folk's feet on the ground for centuries, but not your adrenaline-junkie record breaker ...

The Birdman of Norway

http://y2u.be/ER1PGYe9UZA

Is it a bird? Is it a plane? No. It's Espen Fadnes, the World's Fastest-Flying Human Being. In his flying-squirrel suit, Norwegian Espen routinely leaps off buildings, bridges, mountains and cliffs – and flies. Winning a base-jumping competition in 2010, he officially became the fastest-flying human. Just watch as he calmly (although, to be fair, he admits he's completely terrified) steps off a 4,068-foot (1,240-metre) cliff in Stryn, Norway, and flies through the air at speeds of over 150 mph (250 km/h).

Jump de Triomphe

http://y2u.be/MLejkyXbJlc

Australian motorcycle stunt rider Robbie Maddison likes a New Year's Eve party; his record-breaking end-of-year stunts have become a tradition for the thrill-seeker. Few of them can beat the 2008 effort when the 27-year-old sped his bike off a 35-foot (10-metre) high ramp to the top of the 96-foot (30-metre) high replica of the Arc de Triomphe in Las Vegas. Having set the world record for the highest motorcycle jump, he then plunged the 80-foot (24-metre) drop back – breaking his hand in the process.

THE FASTEST BARE-HAND CLIMBER

▼ Look Mum, Just Hands!

http://y2u.be/Wy3SuhEQHVg

Dan Osman was the fastest bare-handed speed climber in the world. In this ascent, he climbs Bears Reach, a 400-foot (122-metre) rock face of Lover's Leap in California, in just 4 minutes, 25 seconds. He uses no ropes or grips, just gaining hold with his feet and his bare hands. Osman held other mountain-stunt world records, including a freefall rope jump of 1,100 feet (335 metres) at the Leaning Tower in Yosemite, California. Sadly, this was also the spot where he met his death after a tragic rope malfunction.

Skyfull

http://y2u.be/SJZ1b8-M4T4

The skies were alive in Arizona in 2017 as the Sequential Games welcomed sky divers from around the world. A few records were blown sky-high, but none more impressively than this mass dive in which 217 sky divers leaped simultaneously from 10 different aircrafts at an altitude of 19,000 feet (5,791 metres). Hurtling to the ground at a speed of 120 mph (193 km/h), they somehow came together from all across the sky, linking up in a giant snowflake-shaped pattern. Suddenly, they were changing positions, the view from above similar to a human kaleidoscope, to become the largest ever group to complete two and three different formations while free-falling.

THE LARGEST MASS SKY DIVE EVER

▲Walking the Walk

http://y2u.be/9W0umbacmzg

In China, Adili Wuxor is known as the "prince of tightrope walking", so his special skill won't be a surprise. The feat itself might impress, though. The 45-year-old Wuxor breaks his own record by walking a wire that's 5,905 feet (1,800 metres) long and about 590 feet (180 metres) above the ground across the Yellow River. He pauses at the centre for over half an hour, performing various stunts on the 1.5-inch-thick wire (3.6-centimetre) as he waits for his assistant, who started at the other end. He then proceeds to walk over him and continues his epic walk to the end of the wire.

COOL CONSTRUCTIONS

The world of engineering deserves a special mention in the record-breaking hall of fame. The world's greatest tunnels and bridges are spectacular examples of human achievement.

▶ Bridge of Size

http://y2u.be/WP1rZrB9SZI

Opened in 2009, the Sidu River Bridge in Hubei Province of China is the highest bridge in the world. It is a suspension bridge that hangs a vertiginous 1,600 feet (496 metres) above the river gorge. It spans just over 5,000 feet (1,5124 metres) across the river valley; far enough that builders had to use a rocket to string the first pilot line. Some claim it is also the only bridge in the world high enough for a person to reach terminal velocity if they were to jump off.

THE WORLD'S HIGHEST BRIDGE

◀ High and Mighty

http://y2u.be/xIS1ESJ4cOo

"The height of the statue is to remind the youth that the future of the country will be as huge as this," said Indian Prime Minister, Narendra Modi, as he unveiled this 600-foot (182-metre) effigy of independence campaigner Sardar Vallabhbhai Patel. The bronze-clad figure of Patel is twice as high as the Statue of Liberty and dwarfs its nearest rival, the 420-foot (128-metre) High Spring Temple Buddha in China. However, its record is threatened by another Indian construction, the 695-foot (212-metre) memorial to Chhatrapati Shivaji, which is due to open in 2021.

▲ Ice Crystal Maze

https://youtu.be/eosHKfPAljk

The record for the world's largest snow maze goes to Clint Masse and his family, who built theirs in the small town of Saint Adolphe in Manitoba, Canada. Before it melted, their enormous maze covered an area of 30,022 square feet (2,789 square metres). The walls were 2 feet (60 centimetres) wide and 6 feet (1.8 metres) high, which apparently made it quite cosy inside, but even so you probably wouldn't have wanted to get lost in it for too long as the outside temperature was minus 40 degrees!

Little Big Town

http://y2u.be/O8TsKEtR8VQ

Welcome to Casey, Illinois, just a three-hour drive south of Chicago, USA. It might only have a population of 3,000 but this little town is onto a big thing. In 2011, local man Jim Bolin made a 56-foot (17-metre) wind chime to draw business to his wife's tea shop. He and other town folk then crafted a golf tee (29.5 feet/9 metres), wooden shoes (12 feet/3.6 metres wide), a pitchfork (60 feet/18 metres long), a rocking chair (55 feet/17 metres), a mailbox (33 feet/10 metres), and set of knitting needles (13 feet/4 metres) with crochet hook (6 feet/1.8 metres) – all world-record-sized!

THE MOST-DANGEROUS TUNNEL

◣ Cliffhanger

http://y2u.be/GzJnOrr5RUE

Located in the Taihang Mountains of China, the Guoliang Tunnel is deemed the World's Most Dangerous Tunnel. In 1972, inhabitants of the village of Guoliang dug a tunnel 3,937 feet (1,200 metres) long through the rocky cliff. When opened to traffic it was soon dubbed "the road that does not tolerate any mistakes". A tight squeeze for even one vehicle, it twists and turns past 30 or so "windows", which provide views off the precipice to a tumbling abyss hundreds of feet below.

WILD RECORD BREAKERS

Another scan of the great achievers of the wild world brings forth the slow-motion sloth, the aggressive ant, the super-sized sheep and a rather disgusting beetle.

▼ Shell Shock

https://youtu.be/6YAXn5sZvjE

Jonathan's claim to fame – and it's a significant one – is that he's the oldest living land animal in the world. He's a tortoise, originally from the Seychelles in the Indian Ocean, and he's a minimum of 185 years old. We know this because he arrived on the remote Atlantic island of Saint Helena 185 years ago, but what we don't know is how old he was when he first plodded off the boat. Unsurprisingly, Jonathan's faculties are beginning to fail him – he's blind and has lost his sense of smell – but he's still going strong.

THE WORLD'S SLOWEST ANIMAL

▲ Sloth Motion

http://y2u.be/OTp8W251aiQ

The three-toed sloth doesn't do anything in a hurry. It likes to sleep for around 10 hours a day, come down from its tree once a week to do its business and occasionally have a (slow) swim. These are the World's Slowest Mammals, averaging a distance of only 0.15 miles (0.24 kilometres) an hour, with a top speed of 6.5 feet (1.98 metres) a minute. They are so slow that algae grow on them. They do, however, have a good excuse; their long claws, ideal for tree life, make walking particularly uncomfortable.

▶ A Dung Deal

http://y2u.be/I1RHmSm36aE

Forget the gorilla or the rhino – the strongest creature on the planet rolls poo into balls and takes it home for supper. The dung beetle is the world's strongest insect and out-muscles every other animal. Dung beetles can pull 1,141 times their own body weight. This is the equivalent of an average person pulling six double-decker buses full of people. Their incredible strength is, of course, useful for pushing those balls of faeces, but also for pushing out rivals trying to enter their under-dung mating tunnels.

THE WORLD'S STRONGEST ANIMAL

◀ Woolly Sweater

http://y2u.be/kHu-r4gx2kI

Ramblers in Mulligans Flat Woodland Sanctuary outside Canberra, Australia, came across an extraordinary creature. It was the size of a small car and as woolly as a Yeti – it was Chris: a lost and very overgrown merino sheep. The world's woolliest sheep was in a bad way and, carrying five times his normal coat, it's doubtful if he would have survived the fierce heat of the Australian summer. However, shorn of almost half his body weight, Chris was found to be in surprisingly good health and he yielded 89 pounds (40 kilograms) of wool – the equivalent of 30 sweaters.

SPECTACULAR SCIENCE

Making new discoveries and inventions and exploring deeper and further than ever is the business of the scientist. So it is no surprise that they set some pretty incredible records.

Laser Focus

https://youtu.be/TF0tUbwUcCY

There's no science here. There's no long list of features. This is simply an illuminating demonstration of what the world's strongest handheld laser can do – and it's pretty cool. The laser itself is shiny and sleek, and looks just like a prop from a classic sci-fi movie. It's so powerful it can cause matches to burst into flames, and it can also puncture a football, burn holes in a mobile phone and put on a seriously spectacular light show – electrifying!

▼ Goodbye Moon

http://y2u.be/TU6QzMltdZA

Only 12 men have even taken a step on the Moon. Just three years after Neil Armstrong's first great step, Eugene Cernan prepared to climb back into *Apollo 17* as the last man on the Moon. While there, Cernan set the land speed record in the Lunar Rover, 11.2 mph (18.0 km/h), and spent a longer time than anyone else on the lunar surface. "When I pulled up the ladder," he said. "I knew I wasn't going to be coming this way again."

THE LuNAR SuRFACE LAND SPEED RECORD

▲ Do the Math!

http://y2u.be/aSg2Db3jF_4

The Mandelbrot set is a pretty complex mathematical concept that you can look up at your leisure – good luck with that! Mathematicians are still trying to solve some of its mysteries so, if you think you're going to get a simple explanation here, think again! In the meantime, have a look at this because it's awesome. The zooming in on an infinite process creates a mind-blowing set of swirling colourful images, rather like diving into an endless psychedelic pool. This is the record number of iterations, which makes this visual feast well worth including in this book.

RECORD NUMBER OF ITERATIONS

▶ Leading Light

http://y2u.be/3bIXUBXj070

Clever Chinese scientists have created the world's lightest solid material – a graphene aerogel that is seven times lighter than air and 12 per cent lighter than the previous record holder. The sponge-like matter, made of freeze-dried carbon and graphene oxide, is also the thinnest material ever made – a pile of 3 million graphene sheets stands just 1/32 of an inch (1 millimetre) high – but its unique structure also makes it very light and strong. In fact, the claim is that a single sheet as thin as Clingfilm could withstand the weight of an elephant.

LIGHTEST SOLID MATERIAL IN THE WORLD

UNLIKELY CELEBRITIES

The millions of YouTube viewers can create the most unlikely celebrity record breakers. Among the surprising super-achievers are a scooting dog and a bunch of dancing hardened criminals.

▼ Exercise Yard

http://y2u.be/vsG1_eee9fg

The Philippines prisoners' dance to "Thriller" was a YouTube hit and is still worth viewing, but this full-body resistance workout by prison inmates in Peru broke their world record for the most people dancing in a prison. The colourful display was the result of three months' practice by around 1,200 prisoners at the overcrowded Lurigancho prison in Lima. The workout saw the prisoners – many of them murderers, drug barons and other serious offenders – strutting their stuff to the sounds and the beats of reggaeton and merengue.

MOST PRISONERS DANCING EVER

▲ Quick Hit

http://y2u.be/0E00Zuayv9Q

"I have a pen. I have an apple. Apple-pen! I have a pen. I have [a] pineapple. Pineapple-pen!" Oh, you mock now but, once you hear it, you'll be singing it all day long. The song "Pen-Pineapple-Apple-Pen" by Piko-Taro, a 40-year-old Japanese DJ, tapped perfectly into the winning formula of catchy lyrics, a memorable beat and a hilariously simple dance routine. His YouTube video has now garnered more than 100 million views, his Facebook video has had 70 million views, and his single – a mere 45 seconds in length – became the shortest song ever to make the Top 100 in the US.

Amazing Afro

http://y2u.be/65-He8_sb_k

Fourteen years ago, inspired by an old photo of her mother sporting an afro hairstyle, Aevin Dugas from Louisiana, USA, swapped her straight locks for her own natural round style. Now she sports the world's largest natural afro, measuring 4 feet 4 inches (1.32 metres) around and 7 inches (17cm) tall. It takes two days to wash and dry her afro and she sometimes struggles to see out from it, but she does admit it makes for a really comfortable pillow.

▼ Dog on Wheels

http://y2u.be/qKYryJ_1poQ

He's a three-year-old French sheepdog with a special talent. Ever since he was a puppy, Norman has been climbing on board a scooter and propelling himself along. Norman balances himself on the scooter with his two front paws on the handle and a back paw on the scooter. He uses his other hind paw to push himself forward. Having already earned the moniker "Norman the Scooter Dog", he then scooted 100 metres in just over 20 seconds – a world record for a dog on a scooter!

Big Mouth Strikes Again

https://youtu.be/ODvYFhNHi78

It's a guess, but Jim Mouth probably wasn't born with that name. By golly he has earned it, though. Jim loves breaking records and many of them come from a dislocated jawbone that opens an awesome canyon between his lips. He's smoked 41 cigars at the same time, lit up 159 cigarettes, held 18 hot dog sausages in there and crammed in 280 straws. This one is his festive feat performed with a Santa hat and clown nose; so just how many candy canes do you think he can he squeeze into that massive pie-hole?

BEST CANINE ON A SCOOTER

WORLD OF WONDER

Movie star George Clooney famously said, "I go on YouTube when somebody says to look something up." I wonder if he found any of these fabulous clips?

▲ Carpet World

http://y2u.be/RhJXARUTZPM

Each year during the holy week preceding Easter, "sawdust carpets" line the city streets in Guatemala. Made of fine, brightly coloured sawdust with dried fruit, flowers and bread, they create an incredible street art of varying and often intricate design. In Guatemala City in April 2014, the longest-ever sawdust carpet was laid. Using an estimated 54 tons of dyed sawdust, it measured 6,600 feet (2,012 metres) long – but in days was trampled away by religious processions .

▼ You Know Who

http://y2u.be/EDQqEJWOUH4

In August 2017 a Welsh schoolgirl aged just 13 was named the world's biggest *Doctor Who* super-fan. Lily Connors fell in love with the timelord when she was just three years old. What began as a few second-hand action figures passed on by her father became an astonishing collection of 6,641 items of *Doctor Who* memorabilia. Through pocket-money purchases and gifts from family, friends and even *Doctor Who* actors, her collection includes figurines, sonic screwdrivers, posters and – in pride of place – a Tardis wardrobe made by her father and signed by the 12th Doctor, Peter Capaldi.

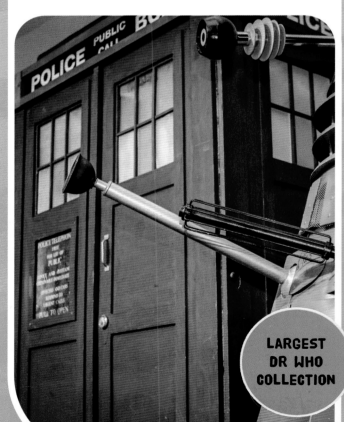

LARGEST DR WHO COLLECTION

▼ Thinking Inside the Box

https://youtu.be/v-mnXV_PowM

Unboxing is arguably the most unlikely YouTube phenomenon ever. Millions click on videos just to watch someone else unwrapping something they themselves want. When a video of a small boy unpacking a Spider-Man battery-powered car got over two million views, the Volvo marketing department had an idea: why not make a video of a little lad unboxing a real-life, huge eighty-foot long truck? Genius! The resulting video is fun and rather charming, and features the world's largest unboxing – even if it is still a million views behind the Spider-Man car.

WORLD'S LARGEST UNBOXING

A Lot of Nerf

http://y2u.be/57MKxz4pJKE

"Nerf or Nothin' – Accept No Substitutes" runs the slogan for Hasbro's Nerf Blaster toy gun. This, however, is one substitute that's rather tempting. Former NASA engineer Mark Rober got together with YouTubers the Eclectical Engineers to construct the world's largest Nerf Gun. The shooter, which looks remarkably like the real thing, is around 5 feet (1.5 metres) long. Powered by a paintball air tank, it can shoot plastic darts at around 40 mph (64 km/h) from a distance of over 325 feet (100 metres). It might be a little bulky for a school bag, but you'd have no trouble from the class bully!

◀ Out of this World

http://y2u.be/E-mR4LCi9nk

A long time ago, in an era far, far away, a special movie spawned a whole array of related merchandising. In 1977, Steve Sansweet was working at the *Wall Street Journal* and came across a promotional book for an upcoming film called *Star Wars* – it began a lifetime obsession. The film generated a myriad of associated products and Steve began to collect them. Now housed in a 9,000-square-foot (850-square-metre) facility an hour north of San Francisco named Rancho Obi-Wan, his display – the biggest *Star Wars* collection in the world – numbers around 90,000 items with another 200,000 or so in storage awaiting classification.

▼ It's All Relative

http://y2u.be/WebTR66FJPc

Sect leader Ziona Chana has 39 wives – all sharing a 100-room mansion in a holy village in India. The largest family in the world lists 32 sons, 18 daughters, 22 grandsons, 26 granddaughters and seven great-grandchildren all living under one roof. While the youngest wife gets the bedroom next to Ziona, the eldest wife runs the household and organizes the meals, which can see them preparing 30 chickens, peeling 130 pounds (59 kilograms) of potatoes and boiling more than 200 pounds (91 kilograms) of rice.

THE LARGEST FAMILY IN THE WORLD

PEOPLE POWER

One day in the far-flung future, everyone will hold a record for something. These guys have already made their mark, but there's a record out there for everyone …

Off His Trolley

http://y2u.be/HcCoVFhdO3g

This crazy record-breaking invention is guaranteed to make the trip to the supermarket a lot more fun. Rodney Rucker of Arizona, USA, has created a shopping trolley 16 feet (4.8 metres) tall and V8-powered – the largest motorized shopping cart in the world. This fantastic vehicle sits six people comfortably in the basket, with another person behind the wheel in the "child's seat". The trolley can comfortably cruise along at 60 mph (96 km/h), but it's probably best not to do that down the frozen-vegetable aisle.

▼ Antenna Man

https://youtu.be/NivuCuwZ944

Cyborgs – part-people, part-machines – are the stuff of science fiction films, but Northern Irish artist Neil Harbisson is the first person to be legally recognized as a cyborg: his passport even says he's one. Neil was born completely colour blind and sees the world in shades of black, white and grey. In 2004 he convinced a doctor to implant an antenna into his skull. Called an "eyeborg", it converts colour into vibrations that his brain can interpret. A far cry from scary fictional cyborgs, Neil looks just like a normal person – just a normal person with an antenna.

▶ It's a Twister

http://y2u.be/DwL993LKsFU

Most of us remember going head over heels. Tuck your head in and propel yourself forward. Well, Liu Teng, China's most flexible woman, does something similar – but almost back to front. The 24-year-old, often called the "Queen of Contortion", already held jaw-dropping records for an extreme back-bend off the edge of a table and using her foot to pick up a drinking glass, as well as for the fastest time to travel 65 feet (20 metres) in a contortion roll. In 2017 she broke her own record for the latter in a quite extraordinary and elegant movement.

▶ Heads Up, Bro!

http://y2u.be/At6YhanMLz0

Fans of TV's *Game of Thrones* might recognise the setting for this record as the Great Sept of Baelor. It is, in fact, the Cathedral of Girona in Spain, where Vietnamese circus artists Giang Quoc Co and Giang Quoc Nghiep chose to perform their amazing world-record head-to-head balancing act. The acrobats climbed 90 of the picturesque steps of the cathedral in one minute with one brother balanced on top of the other, using only head-to-head contact. It wasn't the time for the brothers to fall out and, fortunately, they kept clear heads and held any sibling rivalry in check.

WORLD'S BEST BALANCERS

▶ High Kicking

http://y2u.be/sL4xS2t2Yk0

Twenty-three-year-old Canadian Silvana Shamuon is no novelty act. Silvana has been practising martial arts for over 17 years. She received her junior black belt at the age of 11, was inducted into the Universal Black Belt Hall of Fame in 2007 and represents her country in international tournaments. So, for a bit of fun, Silvana attempted the world record for the most items kicked off people's heads in one minute. Students from her old high school lined up wearing American football helmets fitted with kicking tees and footballs. Needing to beat 67 for the record, Silvana wound up her powerful kicking leg…

▼ Bearded Woman

http://y2u.be/rgQjfcpG7XY

After enduring years of bullying, 25-year-old Harnaam Kaur turned herself into a body-confidence advocate, model and Instagram star. The brave story of the youngest woman to have a full beard is an inspiring one. Diagnosed with polycystic ovaries, Harnaam has had facial hair since the age of 12. She suffered abuse and threats but, at the age of 15, decided to stop hiding and confront gender stereotypes. She never looked back. As she told the *Guardian* newspaper, "They can try to make a freak show out of me, but my voice and my message [are] much stronger than that. I have power in my voice."

RECORD-BREAKING ROBOTS

Science fiction doesn't seem to stay in the films and books for very long these days. Drones are everywhere, maybe keeping a close eye on the dancing robots in the record books.

Massive Spider-bot!

https://youtu.be/iUBd35sBMqc

No, it's not a CGI movie monster – it's a real-life giant metal spider. Mantis, the world's largest rideable hexapod, is the creation of Matt Denton, a British animatronics engineer who has worked on the *Harry Potter* and *Star Wars* movies. A massive and terrifying six-legged "spider" robot, it is 16 foot (five metres) long, nearly 10 feet (three metres) wide and weighs nearly two tons. At just 0.62 mph (1 km/h), Mantis might be a slow-mover, but the driver can control a wide range of movements with two three-axis joysticks and 28 buttons. Coming to a nightmare near you very soon!

▼ Eye in the Sky

https://youtu.be/aOd4-T_p5fA

Up, down, left, right… No matter where you look these days, drones are never far away. They have become our eyes in the skies. In November 2015, Intel Corporation lit up the skies above the Flugplatz Ahrenlohe in Tornesch, near Hamburg, Germany, with 100 small drones flying in fantastic formation. A year later, in November 2016, they went one better – or 400 to be precise – with 500 drones all controlled by one pilot. Acting as one, they created a stunning Technicolor light show as dazzling as any fireworks display. It's unbelievable, and earned Intel a Guinness World Record for most unmanned aerial vehicles.

LARGEST DRONE SWARM

▼ Do the Robot

http://y2u.be/QfocjOJrm3c

Not happy just to take our jobs and drive our cars, robots are now threatening to make boy bands obsolete! Just watch these knee-high Dobi robots go as 1,069 of them set a record for the most robots dancing simultaneously. The nearly perfectly executed dance, which took place in Guangzhou, in China, was managed via a central control system and saw the diminutive automatons get on down in perfect time. Some might find it a little spooky but at least when the robots take over, we can be sure they know how to party!

WORLD'S BEST ROBOTIC DANCERS

Robots, Skips and Jumps

http://y2u.be/HT8BvtfG8w8

ULTIMATE SKIPPING ROBOT PENGUIN

Meet Jumpen, quite possibly the cutest robot ever – although that's not his official world record. Jumpen, a big-eyed blue-and-white robot penguin, was built at the National Institute of Technology Nara College, in Chiba, Japan. He was the outstanding winner of a skipping competition at a robot convention in Tokyo. For each skip to count, the rope had to complete a 360-degree revolution and be cleared by Jumpen. By the time 60 seconds had elapsed, the diminutive electronic being had completed a world-record 106 skips, successfully clearing the rope every single time. Altogether now, awwww!

SEEING IS BELIEVING

How often do you hear or read of a record and think, "Surely that's just not possible." If only you could see for yourself …

RECORD-BREAKING BONFIRE

Miniature Machine

http://y2u.be/cSg-yFZ7y0A

In the UK it's called a Heath Robinson contraption, while in the US they call it a Rube Goldberg machine. In France it's an *usine à gaz* (gas refinery), but the Germans come closest to describing it, calling it a *Was-passiert-dann-Maschine* (what-happens-next machine). This video features the smallest ever of these complex devices. Made with incredible precision for an advert for Japanese watch company Seiko, this intricate and beautiful machine uses 1,200 mechanical watch parts, some of which are smaller than a millimetre in size. In action, it's mesmerizing and rather magical.

◀ Norwegian Wood

www.youtube.com/watch?v=fXtSlEW1XmE

Alesund in Norway, a town just 280 miles (455 km) from the Arctic Circle, has a long tradition of celebrating mid-summer with an almighty bonfire. In 1904, one out-of-hand fire burned the town to the ground. This did not discourage the townspeople, though, and every year they continue to pile wooden pallets into a massive bonfire which is lit by a brave soul climbing to the top. The tallest of their incredible infernos was this record-breaking bonfire in 2016 which stood 155 feet, 5 inches (47 metres) high and burned for two days.

► There's the Catch

http://y2u.be/7J4xw_g-WsA

Juggling. No! Don't skip this one straightaway. It's short and really impressive. Dutchman Niels Duinker is no children's party juggler; he's a multiple-record-holder and a serial champion in his field. Niels, whose show is entitled "Gravity is a Joke", has been juggling since the age of 12 and claims to have spent over 15,000 hours honing his craft. It seems to be time well spent too. In 2015 he set the bar for the cup-juggling world record at 12 cups. Then, in October 2017, he went two better. Awesome.

▼ Flying Bum

http://y2u.be/CWiRZXW8t5I

Just why they call it the "Flying Bum" you can judge for yourself. The *Airlander 10*, part plane and part airship, is the world's largest aircraft. It's enormous: 302 feet (92 metres) long – about 50 feet/15 metres longer than the biggest passenger jets – with a cargo capacity of 10 metric tons. The aircraft is eco-friendly, silent, capable of a speed of 90 mph (148 km/h), and is able to land on practically any terrain. It can remain airborne for up to five days on manned flights, but can also float, unmanned, for weeks at a time.

On the Ball

http://y2u.be/GXsacavxteM

There doesn't have to be a point! That's the mantra of Great Ball Contraption (GBC) enthusiasts. A GBC is a machine that receives balls from one module and passes them to another module, rather like a bucket brigade (or the final contraption in the game Mousetrap). In a hotly contested competition, Maico Arts and Ben Jonkman won back their record for the world's largest Lego GBC with a madcap system of a hundred inter-connected lifts, slides and chutes. To give you an idea of quite how complex the contraption course is, it takes the ball 16 minutes and 30 seconds to travel from start to finish.

COOL CAR STUNTS

Car stunts are some of the most exciting clips on the site. These drivers risk life and limb to perform incredible record-breaking tricks and skills on four wheels.

▶ Wheelie Something

http://y2u.be/ggVpCOT9ZqY

Pulling a side-wheelie (driving on just one front and back wheel) in a car is a technically difficult and ludicrously dangerous feat. To drive along on two wheels at breakneck speed is taking it to another level. The speed record on two wheels was last set in 1997, so hats off to Finnish stunt driver Vesa Kivimäki, who finally broke the record in October 2016. Driving a BMW 330 fitted with tyres specially developed by sponsor Nokian, Kivimäki clocked 115.74 mph (186.269 km/h) in his record-breaking jaunt along the runway at Seinajoki Airport in the southwest of Finland.

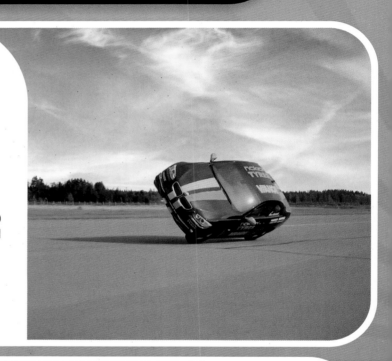

▶ A Hard Truck Story

http://y2u.be/9Jw-TqA4U6I

Why did the 4x4 truck climb the obstacle? To get to the other side, of course! But this was no ordinary truck and no normal obstacle. The truck was a Czech-manufactured Tatra 810, and the obstacle, the Brutt Monster, was the world's highest artificially created obstacle – an extreme steel barrier arcing to 24.6 feet (7.5 metres) high, with a 55-degree incline. It was down to driver Libor Václavík to take on the Monster, a tricky task requiring him to assess the potential of the vehicle, his own driving skills and the laws of physics.

CAR VERSUS WORLD'S BIGGEST OBSTACLE

▼ High Roller

https://youtu.be/9yatAJVA_4E

It's a car ad, so naturally this video is slick, shiny and smooth – but that doesn't take anything away from multi-world record-holding stuntman Terry Grant, who attempts a super-impressive feat: the world's longest barrel roll for a production vehicle. Behind the wheel of a Jaguar E-Pace, Terry not only performs a 50-foot (15.3-metre) long jump, he adds in a 270-degree corkscrew-like roll as well. This was the first time a production car had ever completed such an extensive rotation in this kind of stunt.

LONGEST BARREL ROLL FROM A PRODUCTION CAR

Practice Makes Perfect

http://y2u.be/febbQ4dvjUk

This looks so good. Fabulously shot with in-truck and under-truck cameras and the fantastic setting of a New Mexican ghost town, you almost don't care about the record. Bryce Menzies launches his two-wheel drive truck over the ramp and covers 379.2 feet (115.6 metres), beating the previous record by nearly 50 feet (15 metres). But that isn't the whole story. This jump was only a practice but, just after completing it, he wrote off the truck, fracturing his shoulder in the process. He was supposed to perform the feat on live TV but couldn't. Fortunately it didn't matter because this glorious footage was in the can.

SMASHING THE JuMP RECORD

▼ Ramping It Up

http://y2u.be/L5N7R9Wbe_E

This is the closest you will ever come to seeing a flying car. It was New Year's Eve in Long Beach, California, in 2009, and 20,000 people had come out to see all-action driver Travis Pastrana try something really crazy. Pastrana, a rally champion turned stunt driver, launched his Subaru Impreza STI rally car off a ramp on the Pine Avenue Pier at 91 mph (146.6 km/h). He soared over Rainbow Harbor before successfully landing on a floating barge 269 feet (82 metres) away – almost 100 feet (30 metres) more than the former jump record.

PET RECORDS

These cool creatures have been officially verified as the biggest, sportiest, smallest and most agile.

▶ Monster Bunny

http://y2u.be/SbADYnhHtGg

Darius the rabbit weighs in at three-and-a-half stone (22.2 kilograms) and is the size of a small child. He's the biggest rabbit in the world, but Darius is no freak. His breed, the giant continental, produces large creatures and his mother Alice held the record before him. Five-year-old Darius stretches out to an amazing 4 feet, 4 inches (1.32 metres) long and munches through 4,000 carrots, 120 cabbages and 730 dog bowls of rabbit mix over the year.

THE WORLD'S BIGGEST RABBIT

Who's a Clever Girl Then?

http://y2u.be/unO5whIUF-M

YouTube is full of videos of dogs, and sometimes cats, performing stunts – but Kili the Senegal parrot can match them trick for trick. She claims an unofficial world record by pulling off 20 tricks in just under two minutes. Her feats begin with the customary parrot skills such as rope climbing and nodding. Nothing remarkable there, but carry on watching and you'll see Kili go bowling, match rings to pegs and perform a basketball slam dunk. Worthy of the record books, surely?

◢ Bunny Hoops

http://y2u.be/PWDSKplf9UU

Have you ever seen *Space Jam*, the 1996 movie starring basketball legend Michael Jordan alongside Bugs Bunny, Daffy Duck and other cartoon heroes? No? Well, never mind, watch this instead – the real-life version. Meet Bini the basketball-playing bunny. Apparently, he practices every night, and his commitment and training has paid off. This clip features Bini's world-record attempt for the most slam dunks by a rabbit in one minute – a prize as coveted in the animal realm as it is in the cartoon world.

BEST BASKET- BALLING BUNNY

Dog's Chance

http://y2u.be/68PMF7Xxppl

Alex Rothacker, a professional dog handler from Illinois, USA, takes in dogs that are often on the verge of being put down due to their aggression. Sweet Pea, an Australian shepherd/border collie mix, was one such dog who thrived under Alex's regime. Sweet Pea holds a rather strange record – the most steps walked down backwards by a dog while balancing a 5-ounce (140-gram) glass of water on its head. She achieved 10 and here she even does it blindfolded! Sweet Pea became a celebrity in Germany after appearing on a prime-time TV show, but died a few years ago at the age of 19.

▶ My Little Pony

http://y2u.be/6XQtd9cTGFM

Here's another Einstein. Smaller than most human babies he was just 14 inches (35.5 centimetres) high at birth, weighing only 6 pounds (2.7 kilograms). Now fully grown, Einstein stands 20 inches (50.8 centimetres) high and is officially the World's Smallest Stallion. The smallest horse, Thumbalina, is slightly shorter but, unlike her, Einstein is not a dwarf, he is just a mini miniature horse. He does, however, have a big personality. He has his own Facebook page, has appeared on *Oprah* and even had a book written about him.

THE WORLD'S SMALLEST STALLION

APP APTITUDE

It's the digital age and a new breed of record-breakers – tweeters, texters, vloggers and bloggers – is on the rise. These guys are setting amazing new standards – a bit more impressive than managing to remember your eight-digit password.

Avatar Assembly

http://y2u.be/HPUjg-6nufw

Fans of *World of Warcraft* – the most popular multi-player online role-playing game in the world – were briefly distracted from pursuing quests and fighting monsters to witness a record-breaking diorama. To promote a new expansion of their game at a convention, producers Blizzard created a 1,300-square-foot (400-square-metre) 3D battle, complete with over 10,000 3D printed figures. And just to make the world's largest video-game diorama completely fabulous, every character on the battlefield corresponded to convention attendees' avatars, including their armour, race and weaponry. Great! Now back to the game…

◄ Reality Check

http://y2u.be/yLGMEt3RkAg

There are worse places to spend 36 hours – the dentist, a motorway service station or your aunt's wedding, perhaps? Jack McNee from Sydney, Australia, did his record time in the virtual world. There are many pastimes available on VR, including colonizing alien planets or exploring the ocean, but Jack played *Tilt Brush* for the whole time! With the device strapped to his face for a day and a half, he painted and played *Hangman* and *Pictionary* with his YouTube live-stream viewers. As for eating and comfort breaks, Jack relied on his trusty staff to guide him.

LONGEST TIME SPENT IN VIRTUAL REALITY

▼ Fastest Finger

http://y2u.be/zXjTPnV8ZvM

Fancy a go at being the fastest texter in the world? Here's your chance. Get your phone or iPad set up and see how fast you can type (or swype) the following sentence: "The razor-toothed piranhas of the genera Serrasalmus and Pygocentrus are the most ferocious freshwater fish in the world. In reality they seldom attack a human." Did you make it under 17.5 seconds? If you did, get your claim off to the record-keepers. If not, watch this clip of record-holder Abdul Basit showing just how it's done.

THE FASTEST TEXTER OF ALL TIME

A Man Needs His Nuggs

http://y2u.be/4k1JzcES0G0

In April 2017, 16-year-old Carter Wilkerson tweeted the fast-food restaurant Wendy's asking how many retweets it would take to get a year of free chicken nuggets. The food chain's considered reply? 18 million. Considering that Ellen's famous Oscar selfie generated 3.42 million (the most retweeted of all time), it was a big ask but, when Carter retweeted the message to his 170 followers, saying "HELP ME PLEASE. A MAN NEEDS HIS NUGGS", the response was incredible. The quest captured the public's imagination and Carter sailed past the record. He was still way short of the required total but, nonetheless, Wendy's decently provided the year's supply of nuggets.

SPORTS HEROES

From the sublime skills of Cristiano Ronaldo to the stars of quirky sports such as bog snorkelling or walking on your hands, these people are all record heroes.

MULTIPLE FOOTBALL-RECORD HOLDER

Flaming Flips

https://youtu.be/13colLcrBag

Yeah, fire-breathing… yawn. Hang on, though, this is fire-breathing with a twist – quite literally. In November 2017, on the set of Aussie morning talk show *Studio 10*, extreme acrobat Aiden Malacaria attempted the record for the most fire-breathing full-twist backflips in one minute. Each jump had to be a complete 360-degree backwards flip and, whilst airborne, Aiden needed to perform a 360-degree lateral spin, and blow a flame, without falling. Incredibly he manages ten flame-accompanied flips, two more than the existing record. Someone really should make it a little more difficult!

▼ CR7 Heaven

http://y2u.be/jKb3Pp6YUHg

Love him or hate him, there is no denying the heights that footballer Cristiano Ronaldo has reached. The man they call CR7 has so many domestic and international football records, including scoring in every minute of a game, scoring the most Champions League goals, and being the only player to win every major trophy with two different clubs. In 2017 his three goals against the Faroe Islands saw him pass Pele's record of four international hat-tricks and, the following year, he became the all-time leading international goalscorer in Europe. Are there more records to come? Don't bet against it.

Seconds Out

http://y2u.be/BSp60Y-eLR0

Zolani Tete versus Siboniso Gonya wasn't top of the bill at Belfast in November 2017. The next morning, however, it was the bout people were talking about, even though it lasted just 11 seconds and consisted of a single punch. WBO bantamweight champion Tete was expected to win – just not like this. The 29-year-old South African laid out his countryman, landing a brutal right hook six seconds after the opening bell. The referee officially ended the contest five seconds later as the challenger lay sprawled out. It was the quickest-ever world-title fight in the history of boxing.

▼ Muddy the Waters

http://y2u.be/UoRXZOQBsSQ

The World Bog Snorkelling Championship, first held in 1985, takes place every August at the dense Waen Rhydd peat bog, near Llanwrtyd Wells in Mid-Wales. Bog snorkelling requires competitors to complete two consecutive 60-yard (55-metre) lengths of a water-filled trench cut through a peat bog. Competitors must wear snorkels and flippers, and complete the course without using conventional swimming strokes, relying on flipper power alone. Andrew Holmes is the record holder with a time of 84 seconds.

White Knuckle Walk

http://y2u.be/7i_xFbfptpg

What happens in your lunchtime at school or in the office? I bet it's not as exciting as watching Slava Popov walk around the canteen upside-down, as he does in this clip. The Russian – a former acrobat, and coach to Cirque du Soleil performers – runs a company called Handstand Body Control that teaches fitness through handstand techniques. The fully in-control Slava is a pretty good advert for his company. Watch from two minutes in as he breaks the record for walking on his fists. He covers 108 feet (33 metres) with ease and looks like he could continue down the high street and back.

THE WORLD BOG SNORKELLING CHAMPION

▼ Cheese Chase

http://y2u.be/cvuktushEhY

The Coopers Hill annual event is the oldest cheese-rolling competition in the world. A 9-pound (4-kilogram) Double Gloucester cheese is chased down the hill. The first person to catch it is the winner. However, since the cheese has a one-second start and reaches speeds of 70 mph (113 km/h), this is usually just a race for the finish. Chris Anderson is the most successful competitor ever with 22 cheeses... so far.

CHEESE-ROLLING RECORDS

COOL SPORTS RECORDS

From frantic four-legged running to bionic shoes, the quest for sporting perfection never ends and with it comes the sound of clattering records.

Spiderman

http://y2u.be/vP5Gn6BdTQg

Ready for some real-life Spider-man action? Sport climbing is due to be an Olympic sport in Tokyo 2020 and it should be a real crowd-pleaser. Here's a taster – the 15-metre speed-climbing world record. Czech speed climber Libor Hroza is a star of the sport and shins up the wall in astonishing fashion, skimming 0.12 seconds off his record. Wall climbing is a lightning-fast event so don't blink or you'll miss it. In fact, it's done in a little over five seconds. As one wag says in the comments, "I can't even get out of bed in five seconds!"

FOuR-LEGGED-
SPRINT RECORD
HOLDER

▶ Four Legs Good

http://y2u.be/A3rcWarJOe0

Kenici Ito, a 29-year-old man from Tokyo, Japan, spent over eight years perfecting a four-legged running style based on the wiry Patas monkey of Africa. Neighbours would see him walking around on all fours and he was even shot at by mistake by hunters when training in the mountains. It all paid off in 2012, when Ito incredibly ran 100 metres in less than 20 seconds. He now runs in four-legged races but admits he is still beaten by a fast dog.

Gym Bunny

https://youtu.be/4QuRYaOTIMw

Luis Badillo Jr, aka "King Feet", is said to have the fastest feet in the world. With over 350,000 followers on Instagram, his training videos are legendary. Luis isn't a professional athlete – you need the rest of your body to keep up with your feet! – but he can reach speeds on the gym treadmill which would send most people flying backwards into the rowing machines. These videos of Luis reaching a record 23.5 mph (37.8 km/h) (as fast as Usain Bolt) are made even better by the un-impressed look of the man walking on the adjacent treadmill.

By a Nose

https://youtu.be/LuCpE5CoFtU

Brad Byers is a one-man record book. He's been breaking records for over 20 years with all kinds of scary feats, including the most swords swallowed and twisted, lying on a bed of nails while his brother drives over him on a quad bike and inserting a speeding drill up his nose. Here's one of his records you can try at home. It looks easy at the hands – or nose – of a master, but don't worry, it's pretty safe –as long as you return the cash to the owner!

▲ Going Gaga

http://y2u.be/txXwg712zw4

Lady Gaga has claimed a host of Guinness World Records throughout her glittering career, but she really stole the show at the 2017 Super Bowl. First, she appeared to leap from the roof of the stadium onto the stage in front of her hordes of adoring fans. The pop star then went on to perform the most-watched live musical show in history, with over 150 million people watching her dance her way through her biggest hits during the half-time show. The crowd seemed pretty disappointed when she had to leave the stage so that the NFL match could resume...

WHAT A RECORD!

If God had meant us to fly, he'd have given us wings ... then again, he did give us skateboards, huge swings, dodgy planes and long bungee elastic!

The Only Way is Down

http://y2u.be/JXyQ3N4S5oc

Marc Sluszny is the most extreme adventurer in the world. He's set a world record in bungee jumping, dived with a great white shark and represented Belgium in tennis, fencing, yachting and bobsleigh. In 2012, Marc found a new hobby – running down a building. Here he is completing a vertical run down the side of the Belgacom tower in Brussels. The tower is 335 feet (102 metres) high and he sprinted down the outside of it in a time of 15.5 seconds – a new world record.

▼ Zip trip

https://youtu.be/81ebJIJZ8oI

Velocity 2, the fastest zipline in the world, is sited near Bangor in North Wales. It's really just like the zip ride at your local park – you clip yourself onto the wire and push yourself off the platform and into the air. Except this ride is located on the top of a quarry often shrouded in mist, riders fly over 500 feet (15 metres) above the water, go from 0 to 60 mph (96 km/h) in under 10 seconds and reach a top speed of 125 mph (201 km/h) – and your mum isn't even there to catch you at the bottom!

▶ The "1080"

http://y2u.be/tbjzZHuGTng

In March 2012, at the age of 12, Tom Schaar became a skateboarding legend. Less than a year after becoming the youngest skateboarder (and only the eighth ever) to successfully land a "900" (2.5 revolutions in the air), he landed a three-revolution "1080". He was the first skateboarder to successfully attempt the feat despite many efforts from leading boarders. Tom, who expected to spend all day trying to complete the move, nailed it on only his fifth attempt.

THE WORLD'S FIRST "1080"

▲ Big Rush

http://y2u.be/FrY6OJk-z0I

The Moses Mabhida Stadium in Durban, South Africa, was built for the FIFA World Cup in 2010. The imposing 54,000-seater venue, instantly recognizable from its beautiful white arches, now hosts sports matches, events and the world's only stadium swing – the biggest swing of any kind. Those venturing to the top of the stadium are afforded a fabulous 360-degree view of Durban and a chance to ride the Big Rush Adrenaline Swing. This thrilling experience begins with a 288-foot (88-metre) freefall followed by a massive 721-foot (220-metre) arc that takes the rider into the centre of the stadium. Not for the faint-hearted!

WORLD'S BIGGEST SWING

▲ Flight of Fancy

http://y2u.be/KUIZQ3JyrBM

Man cracked the secret of flying more than a hundred years ago, but you wouldn't think it watching the Red Bull Flugtag. Held annually since 1992 all around the world, the "flying day" event sees participants build and then pilot their homemade flying machines off a 28-foot (8.5-metre) high flight deck. Judged for distance, creativity and showmanship, the aerodynamic qualities of the aircraft are often questionable. Many teams crash pretty instantly and chaotically into the waters below. However, in 2013 the Chicken Whisperers team set a distance record of 258 feet (78.64 metres) in Long Beach, California.

In Full Swing

http://y2u.be/xkqTDtYPuho

Think back to those carefree days in the playground and getting some real height on the swings. Didn't you always wonder whether you could go over the top and complete a 360-degree swing? Welcome to the sport of Kiiking. Invented in 1996 in Estonia, Kiiking sees adults swinging on massive swings with telescopic steel arms that can be extended for each competitor. Although now practised around the world, the record is fittingly held by an Estonian, former Olympic rower Kaspar Taimsoo. Now, you don't see that kind of thing down the park…

LONGEST RED BULL FLUGTAG FLIGHT

HAIR-RAISING RECORDS

There are some special people for whom "doing their hair" doesn't mean a few minutes with a brush and a mirror. Hairstyles, beards, moustaches and other follicular follies are their step to stardom ...

▶ High and Mighty

http://y2u.be/vl3imFyfBU8

You'll know the hi-top fade when you see it. The afro-style haircut – short on the back and sides but big on top – was popular in the 1990s. It was, perhaps, most famously worn by Will Smith in the early seasons of *The Fresh Prince of Bel-Air* and is now enjoying a revival. That won't be harmed by US model Benny Harlem, who broke the Internet in 2016 with pictures of his and his daughter's beautiful and natural hair, and then, a year later, produced a 20.5-inch (52-centimetre) high hairstyle, which broke a world record for tallest hi-top fade.

THE WORLD'S TALLEST HI-TOP

◀ Blow-Dry Bunny

http://y2u.be/iUZgEFRoIX8

English Angora rabbits are the supermodels of the rabbit world, regularly sweeping up the prizes at shows. Looking like a basketball-sized cotton-wool ball, they're incredibly cute and the only rabbit that has hair covering its eyes. Prize-winning Angora breeder Betty Chu has 50 of them, and not only does she take them to competitions, but she uses their wool to knit hats, scarves and mittens. The most famous of them is Francesca, whose sumptuous fur won her the accolade of the rabbit with the longest hair in the world – her coat measured in at 14.37 inches (36.5 centimetres).

THE WORLD'S
LONGEST
MOHICAN

▼ Hard to Handlebar

http://y2u.be/PKzBzDY5I50

Ram Singh Chauhan of India is the proud owner of the world's longest moustache, stretching an incredible 14 feet (4.27 metres). Now 57, he started growing his moustache in 1970. It isn't an easy life – Chauhan spends an hour every day cleaning and combing his moustache, and when it is not on proud display, he has to neatly wrap it around his neck. However, it has brought him prestige and some fame, with appearances in Bollywood films as well as the 1983 James Bond film *Octopussy*.

▲ The Vast of the Mohicans

http://y2u.be/_aYuKyUCTyw

Usually, Kazuhiro Watanabe's hair is clipped up so it doesn't drag around his knees. It has taken the Japanese fashion designer 15 years to grow it that long, but it is all part of his record-breaking plan. When Kazuhiro gets dressed up (usually for an outdoor event), he and his stylists go to work with three cans of hair spray and an entire bottle of hair gel. Just three hours later, he has the world's highest Mohican – a spike that is a massive 3 feet, 8.6 inches (1.13 metres) high.

THE LONGEST
MOUSTACHE IN
THE WORLD

SETTING YOUR OWN RECORD

Even in our wildest dreams, we can't hope to emulate the feats of some of the record breakers in this book. The achievements of Usain Bolt or Cristiano Ronaldo are the result of a talent and dedication possessed by few. Others are born to be record breakers by dint of an exceptional physical attribute – a long tongue, big feet – whether they like it or not! Still, the budding record breaker need not despair. There are plenty of videos in this book to inspire anyone to write their name in the history books.

Perhaps you already have a unique skill or hobby that can rival the record holders. For example, you might have a great talent for skipping or licking your nose or you might have quick reflexes or a steady hand. It is likely that your particular skill isn't yet at the level of the current record holders; most of the achievements in the book are due to practice and hard graft. Start working at it now, though, and who knows what heights you will reach?

You don't have to possess a great physical skill to enter the record books. There are plenty of other entries that are equally impressive. Mental agility is a popular area and there are incredible feats of reading, mathematics and memory; world-beating collections – of anything from TV-show memorabilia to cereal packets – form a fascinating aspect of record breaking; and someone needs to organize the large-scale gatherings that beat records.

If you need to research your goal, go online and check the existing record. Some in this book did just that and discovered it was a target they could aspire to and eventually beat. There are various organizations, including sporting bodies, who keep their own statistics. Most famously, the *Guinness Book of Records* (www.guinnessworldrecords.com) has been keeping records since 1955 and has a comprehensive database and an online application process.

If you are looking to set a more unusual record, it might be worth consulting recordsetter.com, where you will find inspiration and challenges for all kinds of records – many of which can be attempted in your own kitchen or bedroom. If you don't fancy taking on other people's records, you can always invent your own category. You'll definitely have a record, but don't count on keeping it for long – it's a mighty competitive record-breaking world.

INDEX

A Boy and His Atom 101
acceleration and deceleration in a afro hair, largest 127
Ai-Petri, Crimean Mountains 32
aircraft, largest 137
Alberta, University of 48
Alexander, Joe 58
Alonso, Fernando 31
Alves, Rodrigo 26
America's Got Talent 35
Ancona, Mitch 22
animal, oldest 122
animal, slowest 122
animal, strongest 123
ant with world's fastest bite 69
apples, crushing with biceps 29
apples, mouth-held, chainsaw chopped 132
Armstrong, Neil 124
Arnold, Dani 45
Arts, Maico 137
artwork shredded, most expensive 116
athletics, sprinting 17
Attenborough, Richard 101
Avengers: End Game trailer views 12

backflipping 45, 146
backward basketball shot 54
backward rollerskating in stilettoes 54
backward running mile, fastest 48
Badillo Jr, Luis 151
ballast ball surfing 75
balloon, highest altitude sat on top of a 95
balloon-popping dogs 84
balloons, longest kept in air 88
Bania, Kevin 89
Banksy painting, shredding of 116
bare-handed climbing, fastest 118
barrell roll, longest production car 139
BASE jumping 45, 62
Basit, Abdul 145
basketball shots 49, 54
basketball drop, highest 14
basketball, rabbit 143
bass guitar, most strings on a 67
bath bomb, biggest 87
Battista Tocci, Giacomo and Giovanni 25
Baxter, Michael 36
bearded females 133
Beatles 59
bed of nails 72
beer-carrying, most 36
beer mat flipping 87
bees, covering face with 113
Begovic, Asmir 89
Berdimuhamedow, President 80
Biale, Davide 67
bicycle, heaviest 103
Big Freedia 96
biggest bath bomb 87
Big Mac 22
bird call, loudest 21
birds, dangerous 68
bite, world's fastest 69
Blosom (cow) 21
blow torch extinguished on tongue 112
body art 27
body, most flexible 110
body piercings, most 114–15
bog snorkelling 147
Bolian, Ed 75
Bolin, Jim 121

Bolt, Usain 16
bonfire, biggest 136
Booker, Eric 'Badlands' 36
Boruc, Artur 89
bottle flipping, biggest 36
bowling backwards 55
boxing, quickest world-title fight 146
Boyer, Derek 51
breakdancing 111
breath, holding 10
bridge, highest 120
bridges, scariest 32
Britton, Anthony 33
Brown, Broc 24
Browning, Richard 47
Brownlee, Marcus 117
Brussels sprouts, largest helping of 106
BTS 12
bubblegum bubbles 107
Buc-ee's Car Wash 92
buildings, climbing 60
buildings, leaning 61
buildings, running down 152
buildings, tallest 62–3
Bullitt, sale of Ford Mustang GT from 101
burgers, eating 22
burgers, largest 70
burrito-eating, speed 106
Butler, Tom 91
Buzzfeed 88
Byers, Brad 112, 151

Cabañas, Ronald 34
Chan, Calen 44
California, University of, Irvine 48
candles, extinguished by farts 34
Cannonball Run 75
Capital Gate 61
Captain Calamity 76
car flipping 51
car, jump record in 140–1
car, two-wheel record in 138
car wash, longest 92
Carlons, Juan 113
"Carolina Reaper" 22
carpet, sawdust, longest 128
car barrel roll, longest production 139
Cascata del Salto waterfall 9
Casey, IL, large objects in 121
cassowary 68
candles extinguished with nunchucks 97
candles held lit in mouth, most 112
car speed from standing start, fastest 16
cat with most Instagram followers 78
Catrinas, gathering of 27
cats, acrobatic 78
cats, fattest 79
cereal bowl challenge, world's largest 38
Cernan, Eugene 124
Charles, Shemika 111
Charlotte Harbor 18
Chasing Ice 42
Chauhan, Ram Singh 155
cheese rolling 148–9
Chicken Whisperers team 153
chicken wings, most expensive 23
chilli peppers, hottest 22
Chinedu, Harrison 97
Cho, SeungBeom 64

Christen, Georges 73
Chu, Betty 154
chugging soft drinks at speed 36
Circle of Light Festival, Moscow 60
circus skills 14
Chestnut, Joey 107
chopping melons on body 35
Cima Grande, Dolomites 45
cliff jumps 9
climbing, speed 150
clingfilm, wrapping a person in 58
clothes pegs, clipping to face 34
clubs, juggling with 14
cockroaches-in-mouth challenge 57
coffee-bean mosaic 71
coffee cup mosaic, Tutankhamun 93
coldest inhabited spot 43
Colonel Custard 76
Comic Con 41
conductor, youngest orchestra 66
conjoined twins 25
Connors, Lily 128
contortion, fastest moving 132
Corsan, Fraser 8
cow, tallest 21
Cowell, Simon 35
Cowen, Andrew 55
Craig, Daniel 33
Creme Eggs, fastest eaten 106
crochet blanket, largest 76
crocodile, Nile 69
cupcakes, speed-eating 37
cyborg, first human 132
cycling, with football on head 97
Cyrus, Miley 13, 96

da Vinci, Leonardo 71
da Silva Santos Jr, Neymar 117
Dalton, Emma 106
darts, most caught 58
Davidson, Elaine 114–15
Day, Maxwell 105
De Moraes, Ederson 29
Dead Sea 10
Deep Blue (shark) 21
Denton, Matt 134
"Despacito" 12
DiCaprio, Leonardo 100
diet, strangest 86
distance record, Red Bull Flug Tag 153
dive coaster, tallest, fastest, longest 30
Djoos, Christian 81
Dobi robots 135
Dobrik, David 77
Doctor Who collection 128
dodgeball 48
dodgem, fastest 102
dog, most steps walked backwards by 143
dog, on scooter 127
dogs, tallest 85
dogs, ugliest 84
doll-like, most 26
dominoes, longest line toppled 93
Donaldson, Jimmy 86
Dose, Frank 103
Dragon Ball Z 41
dress, most expensive 100
drinking, speed and capacity 36, 37
drones, displays of 134
drop kick, longest 29
drop ride, tallest and fastest 30
Dugas, Aevin 127
Duinker, Niels 137
dung beetle 123
Dyrdek, Rob 55

ears, pulling heaviest weight with 50
eating, competitively 36, 37, 38, 56, 106, 107, 108–9
eggs, balancing 64
Elchyev, Etibar 25
Elegant Death 27
"Elephant's toothpaste" chemical reaction 77
Elmore, Simon 37
elves, Santa's, record number of 82–3
escapology 33
Etnias (mural) 39
explosions, as film stunts 33
eyelashes, longest 105

Face Team Acrobatic Sports Theatre 28
Fadnes, Espen 118
family, largest 130–1
fastest bite, world's 69
fastest drive across USA 75
fastest folk dancing 110
fastest marathon 17
fastest wrapping a person in clingfilm 58
fastest pit stop, Formula 1 52
fastest sofa, world's 102
fastest car speed from standing start 16
fat-tailed scorpion 68
feet, largest rotation of 105
Feig, Paul 80
Felix, Mark 73
Fell, Chad 107
Ferrari World 31
Ferrero, Miguel 90
Fessler, Travis 57
film, most expensive 100
film, most extras in 101
film, smallest 101
film stunts 33
film trailer, most viewed 12
fire running 33
firework, largest 93
fizzy drinks at speed 36
flag, human, largest 81
flatulence to extinguish candles 34
flight, most expensive 116
flipped, most beer mats 87
flipped, most plastic water bottles 87
flyboarders 46–7
flying human, fastest 118
foggiest place in the world 43
folk dancing, fastest 110
Fonsi, Lui 12
football, altitude drop 29
football, balanced on head 97
football, highest-paid player 117
football, international hat-tricks 146
free climbing 45
freerunning course, longest 44
Ford Mustang GT, most expensive 101
"Formula Rossa" 31
Fricska folk dancing group 110
frisbee throwing 65
Fugen, Fred 62
Furious Pete 108–9
Furman, Ashrita 35
Furze, Colin 102

Galyon, Ronnie and Donnie 25
gape, widest 24
Gandhi 101
Gates, Bill 13

Ghostbusters 80
Giang Quoc Co 133
Giang Quoc Nghiep 133
Giant Weta 20
Gillamoos beer festival 36
Glover, Tony 23
goalkeeper-scorers 89
gold-plated chicken wings 23
golf, and highest and longest-par hole 28
golf, long putts 49
Gorillaz 13
Gould, Dean 87
Grant, Terry 139
graphene 125
great white shark, largest 21
Greenspan, Madison 57
Griggs, Nathan "Whippy" 15
Grimsson, Gudbjorn 17
gurning, record and challenge 98–9
Gyde, Stephen 148

hailstones 19
hair, strength of 50–1
hair, tallest hi-top 154
haircut, fastest 65
handstand, farthest walked in 147
Hanglip Mountain 28
Hanks, Tom 97
Harbisson, Neil 132
Harlem, Benny 154
Harlem Globetrotters 9, 49, 54
Harrison, Hammer 9
Hawking, Stephen 13
Hawkins, Jess 26
head-to-head balancing 133
headspins, record number of 111
heaviest load pulled via ears 50
heaviest load pulled via nose 50
Helmke, Chuck 27
Hercules hold record, World's Strongest Man 73
Hershey Bears American ice hockey team 81
Hevesh, Lily 93
highest pogo stick jump 29
High Spring Temple Buddha 120
Holmes, Andrew 147
Honda Mean Mower 26
hot dogs eaten, most 107
hot sauce, drinking 35
How Ridiculous 14
Hroza, Libor 150
human cannonball 35
human cyborg, first 132
human flag, largest 81
"Human Fuse" 35
"Human Ken" 26
Human Tool Box 112
Hurricane Charley Gas Station video 18
hurricanes 18 (*see also* weather, extreme)
Hutchinson, Biff 29

ice balls 19 (*see also* weather, extreme)
iceberg calving 42
Ilulissat Glacier 42
insect, strongest 123
insects, large 20
Instagram followers, cat with most 78
iPhone, most expensive 117
Isaacs, Dougie 88
iterations, number of 125
Ito, Kenici 150

Jackson, Michael 71
Jai Alai 65
Janecek, Rudolf 14
Jaró, Csaba 71
jaws, strong 69
Jayhawks basketball team 66
jet suit, fastest 47
Jianxia, You 105
Johnson, Isaac 24
Jonathan (tortoise), world's oldest
    land animal 122
Jonkman, Ben 137
juggling 14, 137
juggling, fastest cup 137
jump, highest from standing 89
jump, long-distance ramp 139
Jumpen 135

K-Pop 12
kamehameha, most people per-
    forming a 41
Kansas University basketball fans 66
Kaur, Harnaam 133
Kennedy, John F. 100
Khalifa Tower 62
Khris, Taig 44
kick, longest drop 29
kicking items from people's heads
133
Kiiking 153
Kilimanjaro water slide 31
Kinderdijk 111
King of the Onions 23
Kipchoge, Eliud 17
Kivimäki, Vesa 138
Kobayashi 37, 107
Kobra, Eduardo 39
Koenigsegg Regera 16
Kohler, Florian "Venom Trickshots"
38
Kosen, Sultan 24
Koutoupis, Konstantinos 65
Kuhne, Friedi 11

Lady Gaga 151
Langeder, Hannes 103
landslides 19
largest great white shark 21
Lark Harbour 43
laser, strongest handheld 124
Latynina, Larisa 59
Law, Thunder 49, 54
lawnmower, fastest 26
Lazeretto, The White Stripes 67
Leaning Tower of Pisa 61
Lee, Ben 87
Lego ball contraption 137
Lesco, Michelle 56
Liaschuk, Olga 73
Liebian International Building
waterfall 61
lightning, several strikes by 145
lightning storms 43
limbo, beneath a car 111
Lizotte, Simon 65
longest drop kick 29
longest legs 24
Lotito, Michel 86
low-to-ground roller-skating 10
loudest bird call 21
loudest sports fans 66
low-to-ground roller-skating 10, 54

Mandelbrot set, the 125
Marvel comics 41
McCarthy, Melissa 80
McCartney, Paul 59
McDonald's 22
McNee, Jack 144
McQueen, Steve 101
Maddison, Robbie 118
Maddie Rae's Slime Glue 57
"Magnetic Man" 25
Maharana, Manoj Kumar 37
Maier, Michael 21
Malacaria, Aiden 146
Mallie's Sports Grill & Bar 70
Mannequin Challenge 97
mantis shrimp 68
marathon run, fastest 17
Martin, Guy 15
Massa, Felipe 31
Masse, Clint 121
material, lightest 125

mathemetics 125
mayonnaise eating at speed 56
maze, largest snow 121
memory, chimp's 20
Menzies, Bryce 139
Mercado, Kevin "Peg Man" 34
metal objects, attracting 25
Mildon, Jed 45
Milly, smallest dog in the world 84
milk squirting 56
miniature machine 136
Miser, Bryan 35
Mishra, Dipanshu 15
Mitchell, Drew 29
Moffatt, Alastair 54
Mohican hairstyle, highest 155
monowheel, fastest 103
Monroe, Marilyn 100
moon, longest human time on 124
moon, land speed record on 124
moon, longest human time and
    land-speed record on 124
mosaic, largest 71
Moscow skyscraper tightrope
walk 11
motorbike jump, highest 118
motorbike, most men riding 41
mountain climbing, speed 45
Mount, Hua 33
Mount St Helens 19
moustache, longest 155
mouth, biggest 127
Mouth, Jim 127
Moyer, Kyle Thomas 107
muffin, fastest eating of 107
mural, large 39
music, most-watched live show 151

nails, bed of 72
nails, longest 105
Nala, feline Instagram sensation 78
Napoleon 22
natural disaster, greatest 145
Neistat, Casey
Nerf Gun, largest 129
Nintendo Game Boy, largest 39
Norman the Scooter Dog 127
North Yungas Road 32
Nottingham Symphony Orchestra
66
nunchucks, candles extinguished
with 97
Nyad, Diana 90

obstacle, highest artificial 138
oldest land animal in the world 122
onions, fast eating of 108–9
onions, heavy 23
Ono, Aichi 111
Outback Festival 51
Ouvrard, Remi 93
Oymyakon 43

parallel parking 54
Paris Saint Germain 117
parrot, stunts by 142
Pastrana, Travis 141
Patel, Sardar Vallabhbhai 120
Pelz, Dave 49
Persson, Sonny 16
Phelps, Michael 59
pies, most thrown in face 76
Piko-Taro 126
pillow fights 40
ping-pong balls caught with chopsticks, most 35
pit stop, fastest Formula 1 52
plankway, Mount Hua 33
Plawczyk, Edmond 91
pogo stick jump, highest 29
pool-cue, longest 38
Popov, Slava 147
Porsche, slowest 103
Posada, Guadalupe 27
power tumbling 49
prisoners, most dancing 126
projected image, largest 60
pumpkin, largest 70
puppy, world's smallest 84
putting, long 49

rabbit, biggest 142
rabbit, longest-haired 154
radio-play records 59

ramp jumping 55
records, large numbers of 58, 72
Red Bull Flugtag 153
Red Bull Formula 1 team 52
Rhythms of Youth 92
Rice, Angel 49
Rivera, Diego 27
roads, most dangerous 32
Rob & Big 55
Rober, Mark 129
robots, most dancing simultaneously 135
robot, fastest skipping 135
robot spider, largest 134
rollercoaster, speed and acceleration of 31
rollerskating backwards in stilettoes 54
Ronaldo, Cristiano 146
rope jumpers, most 8
rope skipping 48
Ross, Diana 97
Rossini, Bianca 54
Rozov, Valery 45
Rubik's Cube, fastest solved 64
Rucker, Rodney 132
rugby passes, most 29
running marathon, fastest 17
running mile, fastest backward 48
Rush, David 58, 64, 112

"sabring" champagne bottles 22
sandcastle, biggest 61
St Paul Saints 40
Sansweet, Steve 129
Santa Claus, most elves of 82–3
Satish, Gagan 10
"Saturnz Barz" 13
sawdust carpet, longest 128
Sawicka, Joanna 50–1
Schaar, Tom 152
Schaller, Lasso 9
Schemmel, Sean 41
Schlenker, Byron 104
Schlenker, Emily 104
Schoeman, Enrico 35
Schofield, Phillip 73
scooter, longest 74
scorpion venom, cost of 117
scorpions, fatal 68
Scott, Kevin 103
selfie-sticks, long 32
Senatore, Mike 36
Sequential Games 119
Shamuon, Silvana 133
Sharm el-Sheikh 10
sheep, woolliest 123
Shivaji, Chhatrapati 120
shopping trolley, largest 132
show tour, highest-grossing 67
shredded, most expensive artwork
116
Siberia 121
Sidu River Bridge 120
Singh, Amandeep 51
singing, most people in round 80
Six Flags Great Adventure 30
skateboarding, first 1080 152
skateboarding cat 78
skating off tall buildings 44
skipping, with rope 48
skydive, largest mass 119
skydiving slam dunk 9
slackline, longest free solo 11
slide, tallest body 31
slime, largest amount of 57
slowest animal 122
Sluszny, Marc 152
smallest puppy and dog in the
world 84
Smith, Matthew 66
Smith, Nicholas 75
snow maze, largest 121
snow sled, gravity-powered 15
snowboarding speed record 91
soccer, goalkeeper-scorers in 89
soccer, multiple records in 146
socks removed blindfolded, most 64
song, shortest in Top 100 126
songs, and No. 1 hits 59
Sony Pictures 101
spaghetti bridges 71
Spectre 33
speed climbing 45

spider-bot, largest 134
Spidermen, most costumed 41
spinning basketball 15
sport, fastest 65
Spotts, Brian 64
Springsteen, Bruce 97
sprinting 17
sprinting, four-legged 150
sprinting in clogs 29
sprinting on crutches 17
stadium swing, only 153
stallion, smallest 143
Star Wars collection 129
Statue of Liberty 10, 120
statue, world's tallest 120
Stig, The 102
Stock City FC 89
stone skimming/skipping, furthest
88
Stonie, Matt 22
Storms, Tim 75
Strange, Johnny 50
Strati, Saimir 71
straws, most in mouth 37
street painting, largest 92
strength, feats of 50–2, 73
Struempfel, Oliver 36
Sudo, Miki 106
Sullivan, Roy C. 145
supercars 16
surfing, and largest wave 91
surfing Santas 41
sushi mosaics 77
Suurhusen, leaning tower in 61
Swann, Madeleine 33
Swift, Taylor 13
swimming, fastest, unprotected 90
swimming medals 59
Swiss ball surfing 75

Tabasco, drinking 35
Taimsoo, Kaspar 153
tallest man-made waterfall 61
tallest statue, world's 120
Tang Shuquan 98
TED talk, most watched 13
teddy bear tossing record 81
teeth, strength of 73
Teng, Liu 132
Tete, Zolani 146
texter, fastest 145
Theiss, Mike 18
thighs, crushing fruit with 73
Tianmen Mountain, China 33
tightrope walk, longest and highest 119
tightrope walk, Moscow skyscrapers 11
Titanic 100
Tkeshelashvili, Jemal 73
tongues, widest 104
toothbrush, and spinning basketball
15
tornado, widest 42 (see also weather,
extreme)
tractor driving, fastest 15
trampoline basketball 28
trap-jaw ant 69
tsunamis 18 (see also weather,
extreme)
tunnel, most dangerous 121
Turkmenistan 80
Tutankhamun coffee cup mosaic 93
twerking, largest gathering 96
Twinkies, most eaten 107
twins, conjoined 25
Twitter, most retweets 145
Twitty, world's smallest puppy 84
tyre change, fastest Formula 1 52

Uber, longest trip 86
Uhas, Nick 77
Unal, Ilhan 39
unboxing, largest 129
underwater breath holding 10
underwater hula-hooping 35
Urban Endeavors 60

Václavík, Libor 138
Veitch, James 13
Velocity 2 zipline 152
Verstappen, Max 52
video game, largest diorama 144

Vincze, Miklós 71
vinyl record, fastest produced 67
violin, fastest playing of 87
virtual reality, longest spent in 144
V.Squad 77
vocal range 75
Volvo 129
VR video, biggest debut 13

Wallace, Ron 70
walnuts cracked with hands 72
waterfall, tallest man-made 61
water, longest distance driven in 17
water slide, tallest 31
water, sprayed from mouth 37
watermelons chopped on stomach,
most 35
wave surfed, largest 91
weather, extreme 18, 19, 42, 43
Weijun, Li 72
whip cracks, most in two minutes 15
white bellbird 21
White, Jack (The White Stripes) 67
Wilkerson, Carter 145
Williams, Ayana 105
Willoughby, Holly 73
windmills performed, most 111
Winnipeg Goldeyes 40
Winram, William 10
Winslet, Kate 100
Wogan, Terry 49
World of Warcraft 144
World's Strongest Man Hercules
hold record 73
Wuxor, Adili 119

Xie Desheng 97

Yang Yongchun 92
Yankee, Daddy 12
"Yesterday" 59
Yilma, Kirubel 37
Yukon Striker dive coaster 30

Zegeye, Tameru 17
zipline, fastest world's 152
Zlata 110
Yoder, Aaron 48
zombie events 40
Zorbing, fastest 90
Zumanjaro Drop of Doom 30

PICTURE CREDITS

The publishers would like to thank the following sources for their kind permission to reproduce the pictures in this book.

4 AFP Photo/Vano Shlamov/Getty Images, 5 Peter Parks/AFP/Getty Images, 7 Arkaprava Ghosh/Barcroft India, 8 (left) Paulo Whitaker/Reuters, (right) Jarno Cordia/ courtesy of Harvard PR, 9 Fotodive.ch/Wilfried Niedermayr, 10 (left) Arkaprava Ghosh/Barcroft India, (right) Courtesy of William Winram, 11 Marc de Boer/Alamy, 12 (top) Thomas Deco/Shutterstock, (bottom) Everett Collection Inc/Alamy Stock Photo, 13 M4OS Photos/Alamy, 14 (top) Katerina Graghine/Shutterstock, (bottom) Claudia Naerdemann/Shutterstock, 15 (top) Pinpep/Shutterstock, (bottom) Chris24/ Alamy, 16 (left) Jonathan Nackstrand/AFP/Getty Images, (right) Shaun Botterill/ Getty Images, 17 (top) Halldor Bjornsson/Alamy, (bottom) Alex Halada/AFP via Getty Images, 18 Stan Honda/AFP/Getty Images, 19 (top) Shutterstock, (bottom) Universal History Archive/UIG via Getty Images, 20 (top) Leonardo Mercon/ Shutterstock, (centre) Shutterstock, (bottom) Mark Moffett/Minden Pictures/Getty Images, 21-23 Shutterstock, 24 Bettmann/Getty, 25 (top) AFP Photo/Vano Shlamov/ Getty Images (bottom) Drew Simon/AP/Press Association Images, 26 Ken McKay/ ITV/Shutterstock, 27 Shutterstock, 28 muzsy/Shutterstock, 29 (top) Julian Finney/ Getty Images, (bottom) Shutterstock, 30 (left) Lester Balajadia/Shutterstock, (right) PitK/Shutterstock, 31 TowersStreet, 32. (top) Shutterstock, (bottom) ITAR-TASS News Agency/Alamy Stock Photo ,33 Shutterstock, 34 Fred Duval/FilmMagic/Getty Images, 35 (top) Shutterstock, (bottom) WENN Rights Ltd/Alamy Stock Photo, 36 (left) Nils Jorgensen/Shutterstock, (right) Erin Hull/The Washington Post/Getty Images, 37 (top) Drozdowski/Shutterstock, (bottom) Shutterstock, 38 Artem Evdokimov/ Shutterstock, 39. Mario Tama/Getty Images, 40 (top) Shutterstock, (bottom) ZUMA Press, Inc/Alamy, 41 (top) Paul Brown/Alamy Stock Photo, (bottom) Jagadeesh NV.EPE-EFE/Shutterstock, 42-43 Shutterstock, 44 Mark Rolston/AFP/Getty Images, 45 (top) Thomas Senf/Red Bull News Ro/Sipa/Shutterstock, (bottom) Photo by Rauke Schalken with Leica, 46-47 Michael Bowles/Shutterstock, 48 (left) Africa Studio/ Shutterstock, (right) Moviestore Collection/Shutterstock, 49 (top) Angus Murray/ Sports Illustrated/Getty Images, (bottom) Ethan Miller/Getty Images, 50-51 Ray Tang//Shutterstock, 52-53 Mark Thompson/Getty Images, 54 (top) Shutterstock, (bottom) John Robertson/Barcroft Media/Getty Images, 55 (top) Angela Weiss/ Getty Images, (bottom) Shutterstock, 56 Shutterstock, 57 (top) Shutterstock, (bottom) mb123/Shutterstock, 58 dpa/Alamy, 59 (top) DFree/Shutterstock (bottom) Ian MacNicol/Getty Images, 60 East News/Shutterstock, 61 (top) Zhukov Oleg/ Shutterstock, (bottom) Shutterstock, 62-63 Shutterstock, 64 (left) Artem Zamula/ Shutterstock, 64-65 Gaizka Iroz/AFP/Getty Images, 65 (top) Evikka/Shutterstock, 66 Lee Young Ho/Sipa USA/Shutterstock, 67 Picturegroup/Shutterstock, 68 Shutterstock, 69 (top) Shutterstock, (bottom) Zaidi Razak/Shutterstock, 70 Shutterstock, 71 (top) Gent Shkullaku/AFP/Getty Images, (bottom) Obuda University, 72 (top) Shutterstock, (bottom) Vitalina Rybakova/Shutterstock, 73 (top) Vano Shlamov/AFP/Getty Images, (bottom) ZUMA Press, Inc. /Alamy Stock Photo, 74 (top) Geoffrey Robinson/Shutterstock, (bottom) Prathan Nakdontree/Shutterstock, 75 Katherine Frey/The Washington Post/Getty Images, 76 Shutterstock, 77 (top) Shutterstock, (bottom) Science Photo Library, 78 (left) Astrid Stawiarz/Getty Images for Shorty Awards, (bottom) Createthis/Shutterstock, 79 (top) Laurentiu Garofeanu/ Barcoft Media/Getty Images, (bottom) Splash News, 80 Dave Mangels/Getty Images, 81 (top) Chris Ryan/Corbis via Getty Images, (bottom) Press Trust of India, 82-83 Piti A Sahakorn/LightRocket/Getty Images, 84 (top) Josh Edelson/AFP/Getty Images, (bottom) Shutterstock, 85 (top) Matt Writtle/Barcroft Media/Getty Images,(bottom) Barry Bland/Barcroft Media/Getty Images, 86 Mr.Whiskey/Shutterstock, 87 (left) Phil Rees/Alamy, (right) Barcroft Media/Getty Images, 88 XiXinXing/ Shutterstock, 89 (top) PA Images, (bottom) Stacie McChesney/NBC/NBCU Photo Bank/Getty Images, 90 (centre) Shutterstock, (bottom) Yamil Lage/AFP/Getty Images, 90-91 Oliver Morin/ AFP via Getty Images, 92 Imaginechina, 93 (top) Lily Hevesh/Barcroft Media/Getty Images, (bottom left) Mohamed Hossam/EPA-EFA/Shutterstock, (bottom right) Shutterstock, 94-95 Guillaume Souvant/AFP via Getty Images, 96 Ilya S. Savenok/ Getty Images, 97 Petri Oeschger/Gallo Images/Getty Images, 98-99 Imaginechina/ Shutterstock, 100 (left) AF archive/Alamy, (right) Kena Betancur/AFP/Getty Images, 101 (top) Egorov Artem/Shutterstock, (bottom) Paul Faherty/Warner Bros/Kobal/ Shutterstock, 102 (top) Geoffrey Swaine/Shutterstock, (bottom) Simon Stacpoole/ Shutterstock, 103 (right) Laurence Griffiths/ Getty Images, (bottom) Markus Scholz/DPA/PA Images, 104 Ruaridh Connellan/ Barcroft USA/Getty Images, 105 (top) Inga Ivanova/Shutterstock, (bottom) Jack Ludlam/Alamy, 106 Shutterstock, 107 (top) Steve Russell/Toronto Star/Getty Images,

(bottom) terstock, 108-109 Jim Watson/AFP/Getty Images, 110 FOX/Getty Images, 111 (top) Shutterstock (bottom), Ruaridh Connellan/Barcroft USA/ Getty Images, 112 Shutterstock, 113 Kuttelvaserova Stuchelova/Shutterstock, 114-115 Mark Campbell//Shutterstock, 116 (top) Etihad Airways/Getty Images, (bottom) Kirsty Wigglesworth/AP/Shutterstock, 117 (top) Enrique De La Osa/Reuters, (right) Caviar PR, (bottom) Christophe Petit Tesson/EPA/Shutterstock, 118 Shutterstock, 119 (top) Roy Dabner/EPA//Shutterstock, (bottom) VCG/Getty Images, 120 (top) Eric Sakowski, (bottom) Wan Cheuk Nang/Shutterstock, 121 (top) Canadian Press/Shutterstock, (centre) © Raymond Cunningham, (bottom) Shutterstock, 122 (top) Shutterstock, (bottom) Mark Philips/Alamy Stock Photo, 123 (top) Michael Potter11/Shutterstock, (bottom) RSPCA, 124 NASA, 125 (top) Visharo/ Shutterstock, (bottom) Zhejiang University, 126 (left) Geraldo Caso/AFP/Getty Images, (right) Aflo//Shutterstock, 127 Austral Int./Shutterstock, 128 (top) Johan Ordonez/AFP/Getty Images, (bottom) Phillip Maguire/Shutterstock, 129 (top) HAP/ Quirky China News/ Shutterstock, (bottom) Shutterstock, 130-131 Adnan Abidi/ Reuters, 132 (top) Shutterstock, (bottom) Sipa Asia/Shutterstock, 133 (top) Pau Barrena/AFP/ Getty Images, (bottom) Jeff Spicer/Leapfrog Films/Getty Images, 134 Shutterstock, 135 Imaginechina/Shutterstock, 136 Kameel4u/Shutterstock, 137 (top) Kai Keisuke/Shutterstock, (bottom) Justin Tallis/AFP/Getty Images, 138 (top) Nokian Tyres, (bottom) Sojka Libor/Czech News Agency/PA Images, 139 Cristiano Barni/ Shutterstock, 140-141 Garth Milan/Red Bull Photofiles/Getty Images, 142 Caters News Agency, 143 (top) Warner Bros./Everett Collection/Alamy, (bottom) Katie Greene/Bellingham Herald/MCT/Getty Images, 144 (top) Blizzard Entertainment Inc. (bottom) UfaBizPhoto/Shutterstock, 145 (top) theskaman306/Shutterstock, (bottom) Jim Watson/AFP/Getty Images, 146 Marcos Mesa Sam Wordley/Shutterstock, 147 Shutterstock, 148-149 Justin Tallis/AFP/Getty Images, 150 Toru Yamanaka/AFP/Getty Images, 151 Kevin Mazur/Wireimage/Getty Images, 152 (centre) Imaginechina/ Shutterstock, (bottom) Peter Parks/AFP/Getty Images, 153 (top) Big Swing, (bottom) Anton Gvozdikov/Shutterstock, 154 (top) Moviestore Collection/ Shutterstock, (bottom) Steve Shott/Getty Images, 155 (left) Adrees Latif/Reuters, (right) Arkaprava Ghosh/Barcroft India, 160 Ken McKay/ITV/Shutterstock

Every effort has been made to acknowledge correctly and contact the source and/or copyright holder of each picture and Welbeck Publishing Group apologises for any unintentional errors or omissions, which will be corrected in future editions of this book.